PUT ON YOUR CROWN

The Black Woman's Guide to Living Single (. . . *and Christian*)

Sheron C. Patterson

"America's Love Doctor"

THE PILGRIM PRESS
CLEVELAND

This book is dedicated to single women who do not yet know that they are queens.

The Pilgrim Press, 700 Prospect Avenue, Cleveland, Ohio 44115-1100
thepilgrimpress.com

Printed in the United States of America on acid-free paper

10 09 08 07 06 5 4 3 2 1

Library of Congress Cataloging-in-Publication Data

Patterson, Sheron C., 1959–
Put on your crown : the black woman's guide to living single (. . . and christian) / Sheron C. Patterson.
p. cm.
Includes bibliographical references and index.
ISBN 0-8298-1696-8 (alk. paper)
1. Single women—Religious life. 2. Christian women—Religious life.
I. Title.
BV4596.S5P37 2006
248.8'432—dc22

2005029412

ISBN 13 : 978-0-8298-1696-9
ISBN 10 : 0-8298-1696-8

CONTENTS

Foreword

In the popular situation comedy *The Facts of Life,* Kim Fields played the character known as Tootie. Tootie loved to find one of her housemates in a difficult situation so that she could declare her famous line, "Oooo, you're in trouble!" Sister-friends, I feel like Tootie today. You may be single, divorced, or widowed and seeking a man; or you may be married and unsatisfied with your husband. It doesn't make a difference to Dr. Sheron Patterson, a.k.a., "America's Love Doctor." If you are bodacious enough, courageous enough, and brave enough to read this book, all I can say is, "Oooo, you're in trouble!" For within the pages of this book are the authentic, real, and honest facts of life about women.

The Love Doctor is in your house with *Put on Your Crown!* She didn't come to play. She is not trying to be politically correct and she will not permit any side-stepping, dodging, or denials to prevail on this visit. She is as "serious as a heart attack" in the cardiac unit where every woman undergoing a major mental, emotional, spiritual, and relational reconstruction seeks help.

The Love Doctor is making house calls today with the materials on these pages. I pray that you realize just how important it is to have her make this personal visit. She has heard your multiple calls for help. She has seen many private patients. She has held Love Clinics where she has attempted to perform group interventions for hurting and confused sisters and brothers. The virus of hurt that is spreading among sisters has become particularly overwhelming. So the Love Doctor decided to make personal, one-on-one calls in order to diagnosis your symptoms, prescribe advice, and share consultation for aftercare and healing.

The Love Doctor wants to spend time with you—alone, up close, and personal—in the privacy of your homes. She longs to allow you all the time that you will need to bellyache, whine, complain, explain, and detail your case. Then, she's going to go into her medicinal bag and help deliver you from much of your self-inflicted pain! I'm telling you again, "Oooo, you're in trouble!" She brought scalpels, lancets, and some digging instruments to get you past your surface scars and into the very core of your issues with men!

Like a storm, the Love Doctor will stir up, destruct, and rearrange all of your old, faulty, and insufficient thought patterns, beliefs, and myths—all of the thought patterns that have held you down, kept you depressed, and discouraged you in your relationships. After every major period of heaven-sent destruction, there comes the period of reconstruction! This is where God uses human beings and all necessary good to help "victims" see a new view, a better perspective of what they thought was failure, and to obtain a brand-new attitude about their future!

If you are not ready for naked and raw truth, put this book down! The Love Doctor does not come to make suggestions; she is giving orders and taking names. She commands each sister to "Put on your crown!" This is a direct order, for we are children of the Most High Reigning Sovereign God. She directs us to comprehend that "queens are not helpless, hopeless, and fragile females!" So, whatever has fostered your sense of learned dependency upon a man, it is thrown out the window at the very start of your healing session.

The Love Doctor commands us to realize that a queen is a mindset and a queen goes into the "new mind" that comes with salvation and a personal relationship with Jesus Christ. The Love Doctor is straightforward, direct, and blunt as she states, "Regretfully, you may be somewhat narrow-minded and believe that success equals a man in your life. The truth is that men are out of your control. What is in your control is the quality of your life. In your pursuit of the crown, success for you will be accomplishing the things needed to be a queen, namely, deleting those things that prevent or deter your queen status, creating new ways of being a queen, and helping other women to become queens."

Whether you are a "veteran queen," a "rookie queen" or a "queen in the making," there is good news for you within these pages! The Love Doctor has done extensive research, consulted with other specialists in their fields, and held trial clinics and tested her hypotheses. She has offered it all to God in fasting and in prayer.

It has been my gift from God to be in relationship with Sista Sheron. It has been my privilege to be involved with her in ministry to the people of God and especially to the sisterhood. Over the years, it has been my honor to have spent personal times both on the road and in her home as we shared our burden for the healing of our sisters. So when our editor, Kim Martin Sadler, asked if I would write this foreword, it was not a problem for me to say with all honesty, "Oooo, you're in trouble!" I know from personal experience that the Love Doctor is on a God-given assignment to cut deep, to get to the heart of the matter, and to exorcise all former excuses in order to assist every sister reach wholeness and her divine destiny.

My prayer is that the God of Earth, Wind, and Fire, who is the Calling God of the Love Doctor, will speak gently to your spirit, whisper encouragement to your soul, and allow the change that is needed for better tomorrows to be yours! Know that we journey together to the land that will never grow old, where eternal crowns are laid up for us. Remember me, for I'm on the journey with you! Shalom, my sisters. Shalom, from your Sista Linda.

—*The Rev. Dr. Linda H. Hollies, Grand Rapids, Michigan*

Acknowledgments

This book was written by the life-changing power of God. I thank God often for choosing me to serve as an ambassador to the world of relationships. God has been good to me all of my life, and I pray that my life is a testimony in and of itself.

I am grateful to my family for sacrificing afternoons and evenings of fun so that I might complete this project. Robert, you are a gracious and supportive spouse. Robby, your teenage perspective kept my writing fresh. Chris, our battles over computer usage kept my adrenaline flowing. Mom and Dad, I appreciate your kind words of encouragement.

A cadre of wonderful women kept me in their prayers and supported my vision of healthy relationships for all. They never question my latest project; they simply ask what they can do to help. They are Sylvia Dunnavant, Vickie Blocker, LaTonya Celestine, Shante Buckley, Terri Earls, and Dr. Barbara Cambridge.

This project would not have its flavor without REJOICE Radio. I am indebted to the radio genius of Keith Solis who partners with me on Wednesday mornings as we minister to thousands of believers. Program director Willie Mae McIver is a jewel who keeps us all going.

The local Dallas media market also influenced this project immensely. I salute the personalities at radio stations such as K-104 FM, KKDA AM, KRNB FM, K-SOUL FM and 97.5 AM. The television stations of WFAA, and Fox 4 helped to bring the images of my ministry into the homes of even more. Thank you to the *Dallas Morning News* as well for inviting me to write on a regular basis. Thanks also goes to three national publications that feature my writing—*Gospel Today, Precious Times,* and *The Trinity Trumpet.*

I wish to thank Dr. Linda H. Hollies for her fervent support of my writing career and her availability for sister-girl pep talks.

Finally, I thank Christene Howard, my administrative assistant, who supports me in all my endeavors.

Introduction

You are expecting, praying, and waiting for a man to enter your life and become your husband. The time before he arrives is crucial. Don't waste this time feeling anxious. Don't waste it sitting on the sidelines of life straining to catch a glimpse of his arrival. Watching for him won't hasten his entrance. I want you fully engaged in your own awesomeness during this time. Seize these moments of singleness and treasure them. These are the moments, hours, days, and weeks, months and, yes, even years before God sends a man into your life. Excitement is in the air. Enjoy life and celebrate the fantastic woman God made you to be. Don't preoccupy your mind with a man but concentrate on becoming a better you. No, this is not a book on how to become narcissistic. It's a book on how to be a happy African American single woman, when the world says otherwise.

With more than twenty years in relationship ministry and a nationally syndicated radio broadcast, I've earned the title of "America's Love Doctor." In that role I've seen thousands of women who doubt and disparage themselves for not having anyone in their lives. They blame themselves by saying, "I'm too fat," "I'm too skinny," "I'm too old," or "I'm too young." They blame men and make generalizations such as "All men are dogs," "None of them will commit," "He can't keep a job." Eventually their negative beliefs determine their behavior and set them on a course that pushes themselves even further away from the man of their dreams. This behavior starts early. I surveyed 135 fifteen-year-old young ladies about relationships, and 90 percent answered yes to the question, "Is having a man in your life high priority?" This group of high schoolers later told me that they had to have a boyfriend at all costs. This meant that a large portion of their energy, talent, and time was going into the hunt. Thinking back on my high school days, I was a lot like them. I wanted a boyfriend too. The difference is that in today's society, we women risk too much, give away too much, and ravage ourselves too much in the quest to be somebody's girl.

That's what this book is all about. I write to calm the chaos and bring peace to the panic that I see in single sisters' eyes. I write to offer insights that might not have occurred to you. Here you will find no judgmental or condemning comments. I have not written this book because I am better than you. I wrote this book because I am obedient to God. Consider me your pastor/coach on the journey of Christian singleness. God placed an intense anointing on my life in the area of healing relationships. I am drawn to single adults like a magnet. Solely due to the power of God, divine wisdom flows through me to you.

I have liberally sprinkled excerpts from the questions posed by listeners of the REJOICE radio broadcast. I am heard every Wednesday morning on Love Doctor broadcast and the listeners keep me busy answering a variety of questions. Due to the anonymous nature of radio, they keep it real and so do I. I believe that there are no dumb questions. We are dumb for not getting answers to our questions in life. I have also included reactions and comments from Love Clinic seminars that I conducted nationally. Your identity has been preserved. All names, ages, and life situations have been changed. All the names used in the book are purely fictional.

My goal for you is to live the life and look of a queen. I am so convinced that you should be a queen that I refer to you as one in this book. Queens are ruling women with political power. Queens are the most powerful pieces on chessboards. Queens are the focal point of the honeybee nest. Queens are also African American single women who love, protect, and celebrate themselves on the road of life.

This book is not going to be easy to digest or deal with if you are in denial about issues relating to yourself. God told me to write about your silent suffering and your long-hidden disappointments. As I write, I pull back the covers and shine a light on all of it. This light does not bring shame; it brings healing because you and God are responsible for the restoration.

This book will clarify your thoughts about men. I never have been a male basher, I just tell the truth. Knowledge is power, and when we have knowledge about men we will be some fierce sisters. Some of us think we know it all about men, when we really don't. Others of us believe we are ignorant on the topic, when we are not. I've devoted two chapters to those topics in order that you might get a full understanding. I pray that the understanding draws you closer to your heart's desire.

In chapter 1, "Put on Your Crown," I offer the mechanics of being a queen. I take you on a step-by-step plan that, of course, starts with God. It is important to ensure that you create a strong connection with God before you go any further. The chapter goes on to include self-knowledge, valuing the places that we live, and thriving in the workplace. Chapter 2, "Reprogram Your Motherboard," challenges you to remove the "stinking thinking" from your brain. There is so much garbage about men and marriage floating around that it clogs us up. This chapter also includes provocative information about reclaiming your virginity. Try it!

Chapter 3, "Sanitize Your Situation," equips you to clean out your life—just as you would your refrigerator or your closet. I'll show you that there are probably some people in your life who are detrimental to your queenliness. They have got to go! In chapter 4, "Revise Your Reasons," we pause and reflect on the reasons why you want to get married. Obsession is the culprit with many, and like a long limousine, it can drive you out of your mind! We get deep in chapter 5, "What's Really Bothering You?" with a look at psychological issues that most commonly affect us. You see, the distress you are experiencing may not be man related, it could be the result of internal issues.

Chapter 6, "You'd Better Have It," is comprised of the essentials that a queen would carry in her purse. She never knows what she will have to do or say, but she does know that her God is able to supply it all! Some of the contents of the queen bag may surprise you; they include having feet like goats and the ability to take the heat! In chapter 7, "Focus Frankly on Friendships," we examine the role of friends in the life of a queen. Some of us are so overwhelmed or angry or bitter that we don't have time for friends, yet a friend is what we need. Some of us have too many friends and we cannot concentrate on our own agenda.

Chapter 8, "Reach Out instead of Lash Out," is designed to help us understand and relate to men in a positive way. I am woefully weary of all the friction between men and women. I let men speak to you about their feelings and hopefully build meaningful bridges. Chapter 9, "Define, Don't Confine, the Men in Your Life," continues to promote love and happiness with the brothers. Authors William July, Ron Elmore, and John Gray offer insightful advice about how you can understand a man.

Chapter 10, "Delivered from Drama," is the emotional chapter, because six single sisters tell you how they escaped from some of the same vile situations that have you pinned down. The true mark of a queen is that she may go through some tough stuff, but she does not stay there. Chapter 11, "Momma Wants a Man Too," is an ode to single moms. It's tough to take care of you and your children and hope for a man in your life, but it's possible. Chapter 12, "Rules for Role Models," reminds you that if you are a queen, you are a role model for young women. They need to hear, see, and talk to grown women like you to see what they should become. You have an obligation to create future queens.

Each chapter concludes with a prayer and some questions for reflection. Read and be blessed!

1 · PUT ON YOUR CROWN

Put on your crown," I told the group of women assembled for a singles seminar entitled "How to Have a Man in Your Life." I anticipated their reaction. Some looked puzzled and confused. Others were agitated. Eyes were rolling and teeth were sucked. It was about to get hot in there because they saw no connection between putting a crown on their heads and a having a man in their lives! "We came to learn about men, not us," they murmured. Many women do not understand how being a queen is related to having a man in their lives. This disconnect is the primary reason why we experience hardship and suffer so much in our desire for male companionship. We don't realize the urgency of our royalty.

You've got to be a queen regardless of whether or not you have a man. There is no room for negotiation. Either you are on top or you are on the bottom. It's your choice. Either you are the queen or you are the chambermaid. One rules the world; the other washes the floors of the world. Too many of us are accustomed to washing floors. God has something greater than that for us. Life as a queen dictates that you come first. Pick up your crown and put it on! It belongs on your head, not smashed in the back bedroom closet under Christmas wrapping paper or packed away with your high school band uniform in the attic.

There is a crown with your name on it! The crown is the outward symbol of royalty and regality. The crown informs the world of what you already know—that you are a queen. You are a queen all by yourself, not because you are married. Queens are not helpless, hopeless, fragile females. You can help yourself, and have done so over and over and over again—thank you. Queens are self-sufficient, independent women who have enough sense to collaborate when the right man comes along. Queens have victoriously come through hell and high water. Queens have labored through the dark valleys and surmounted dangerously high mountains.

A queen is a mindset. The Word tells us, "For as [s]he thinks in [her] heart, so is [s]he" (Prov. 23:7 KJV). If you think it, you know it. It radiates from the inside out. Your queenly status is not based on what you wear, the style of your hair, or the color of polish on your nails. It is something on the inside that shows up on the outside regardless of your situation or surrounding.

Queens are success driven. You've probably experienced success on your jobs, with family, in the community, and in educational endeavors. Naturally, you want it again in your relationships. Ideally, success should occur in all sections of our lives. It is frustrating when we do not have it in our relationships. Regretfully, you may be somewhat narrow-minded and believe that success equals a man in your life. The truth is, men are out of your control. What is in your control is the quality of your life.

In your pursuit of the crown, success for you will be accomplishing the things needed to be a queen, namely, deleting those things that prevent or deter your queen status, creating new ways of being a queen, and helping other women to become queens.

Maybe you've worn your crown for years; it's had a permanent place on your head. You know how to walk the walk and to talk the talk of royalty. You are what I call a veteran queen, and you are a rare breed. I applaud you. Historically, a single woman was a social pariah.

Rather than wearing a crown, she was forced to wear a badge of shame because she was single. Society said that you could only wear a crown if you were married. Society was wrong. Your crown had luster and shine when you were alone or when he held you in his arms. The veteran queen already knows the ropes. Just don't grow weary doing well. Don't get bitter as you live better. This book will give you an extra boost and a pat on the back. And perhaps you may learn a few new insights about being a single woman.

Maybe you are a rookie queen; that's okay. It's great that you made the move up and into the land of queens. You figured it out in time. So many sisters go through life with their shoulders slumped, oblivious to the facts of their royalty. I see them in my seminars and book signings. They look lost and alone. In this book, I am taking them by the hand and leading them to a new place. To be a queen, you do not have to pledge or go through an initiation process. The challenge is staying there and living up to the new expectations. Resist the temptation to sink into an abyss. Don't look back. If you have had to distance yourself from people who were not going in your direction, have no regrets. You may be experiencing separation anxiety. No worries—affiliate with other queens.

Not quite a queen? It's good to be honest. You are still trying to make up your mind. Perhaps you are weighing your options: be a queen or worry yourself into ulcers over a man; be a queen or allow men to treat you in any kind of way just as long as you can stay together. Let's make sure that you are ready to ascend. If you are content living below your potential, you are not ready to be a queen. If you think men are to be fought over, chased down, and given everything at all costs, you are definitely not ready to be a queen. Choose—and choose well—which you will be. Our society will quickly label you an old maid, single for life, or a loser. But you have the final say. We have all been fed a steady diet that portrays single women as desperate, man crazy, and hostile. But who do you say you are?

Mental baggage may prevent you from traveling with me on this journey. Let's acknowledge it now and deal with it. It's our blockage removal strategy. Someone told you, "You can't be a queen," or "You're not queen material." Someone else told you, "You will never amount to anything," or "You'll never have a man because you are too stupid." Leave this putrid luggage at the door and don't look back.

We are ushering you into a new realm of being. This chapter details the top four traits of a queen. Queens have a connection with God like no other. Queens know themselves. A queen's home is her castle. Queens thrive in the workplace.

QUEENS CONNECT WITH GOD

Queens realize that their power source is Jesus Christ. Without him, there is no power. Queens don't try to fake a relationship with Christ. If they fake it, they cannot really feel it. They possess it and are proud of it. There is no such thing as a "closet religion." They read the Bible and spend time in prayer.

Having a relationship with Christ does not require that you become a pastor or a part-time missionary. It is not the life of a religious zealot. Your relationship with Christ does manifest a new attitude—self-sufficiency. You say, "I can do all things through God who strengthens me." (Phil. 4:13). This replaces the needy, hungry, and desperate woman who hungers for male companionship. When you have Christ in your life, there is abundance. Jesus tells us that he came for this purpose—"I came that they may have life, and have it abundantly" (John 10:10).

Queens need the abundance because they never know in which direction life will turn. Edie had not been a Christian for long, maybe a year or two, but what a difference the relationship with God made in her life. "When my husband died last year, I started going to church with a few of my girlfriends. I never had time for church and God; Bruce and I were busy and into our own things," she explained. "God was something other people talked about, but we were not into the church scene. It seemed like something very crazy to believe in someone you could not see, hear, or talk to. But I tell you the truth, when the grief got a hold of me, I figured out fast that there was no other person on earth to hold my hand and comfort me."

Weekly, I cohost a nationally syndicated radio broadcast. Our topics always deal with real-life issues. One day our topic of discussion was "Living in the World versus Living for Jesus." The phones rang off the hook! A queen in the making called in and commented, "I am a new Christian and a single mom. I heard the topic today and I want to testify. When I was in the world, all I did was chase after men and stay out late in the nightclub. But now that I found Jesus, I don't have to live like that anymore!"

A queen's tangible relationship with Jesus is a centuries-old connection. Throughout the Bible, Jesus reaches out to women, especially single women who are struggling. His care and compassion elevates them to queens. The biblical woman at the well is a prime example of one woman who is having man trouble (see John 4:1–39). Here we find a woman who is not living as a queen, in part due to relationship difficulty. She had a string of unsuccessful relationships, five to be exact, and currently she was living with a man. Jesus saw her failures but he also saw her potential and invited her to relate to him as the long-awaited Messiah. He told her, "If you drink of this water you will never thirst." She marveled that he knew all about her and ran to tell the townspeople, "Come see a man who told me all that I ever did!"

In other instances, the connection with Jesus helps queens endure situations that are potentially depressing—loneliness and a desire for children. Viola was a loquacious workshop participant in Atlanta who explained the whole Jesus thing to a room of five hundred people. "My singleness would not make sense without Jesus," said Viola, a forty-seven-year-old never married woman with no children. "I read the paper, I know about the societal problems that caused the lack of eligible men for me. But I refuse to be bitter about it. I know that God is in my situation. In Genesis 50:20 it says, "Even though you intended to do harm to me, God intended it for good." That means that at any time now God is going to bless me. The blessing may be man, maybe not, but God has been good so far. I won't give up, because I've come too far to turn around now."

To keep your queenly connection with the ultimate power source you have to stay prayed up. Prayer is the best vehicle for connecting with God. Pray with honesty. If you feel good today, pray and say, "God, I feel good today." If you feel lousy, say so too in prayer. God already knows what you are thinking, so you are not fooling anybody. Pray a long prayer or make it a short prayer. You could even pray this inclusive Prayer of Jesus, "God in heaven, hallowed be your name, your kingdom come, your will be done, on earth as in heaven. Give us today our daily bread. Forgive us our sins as we forgive those who sin against us. Save us from the time of trial and deliver us from evil. For the kingdom, the power and the glory are yours now and forever. Amen."

Prayer gives you the ultimate source of confidentiality. There are some secrets that should only be trusted with the one who will never tell. I am reminded of the woman who complained to her longtime friend that the friend never kept any of her secrets. The friend replied, "It's not me that's having problems keeping things confidential; it's my friends who can't keep a secret."

Meditation is an excellent means of connecting with God. Meditation means that you focus your mind on the goodness of God and how awesome God is. Meditation is helpful because sometimes we expend mental energy on unproductive things. It has been said that we often "major in the minors." Those thoughts that center on anger, pain, and rejection can paralyze you. Meditation is all about how God can liberate you and your thoughts. Please do not confuse this with Eastern religions. Christians can and should meditate. Even the psalmist wrote in Psalm 27:4 that he longed to spend time meditating: "One thing I have asked of God, that I will seek after; to live in God's house all the days of my life, to behold the beauty of God and to inquire in God's temple."

Here are some suggestions for mediation. Select a favorite passage of scripture. For example, "I can do all things through Christ who strengthens me" (Phil. 4:13). Sit comfortably. Close your eyes. Breathe in and out. Place the scripture in your mind and let it consume you. Speak it over and over to yourself. Do this for fifteen to twenty minutes. This should be a relaxing and spiritual experience.

Journaling is a third means of connecting with God. Journaling is writing your thoughts on paper and allowing the emotions and feelings to be released at the same time. It is a wonderful means of chronicling your life and expressing your feelings. Sometimes we allow emotions to be bottled up. Journaling gives us expression.

You can use plain old sheet paper that you may have laying around or buy a fancy bond journal from the bookstore. You can pour yourself into those pages and allow the journal to transport you to a peaceful place. You can also track the progress of your life with a journal. Write your problems down, and when God delivers you, look back to see what God provided.

QUEENS KNOW THEMSELVES

Queens possess complete knowledge of themselves psychologically and spiritually. The queen's motto is, "If I don't bother to know myself, why should someone else?" Please discover who God made you to be and the purpose that God has for your life. If you are clueless and aimless, you cannot be a queen. What does a woman who is ignorant of herself have to offer? She is an empty shell waiting to be filled. A real man wants a defined, informed woman. Some women erroneously believe that learning about themselves is vanity or that they will loathe what they find. That's the way Ruth felt. She was a woman without a crown on her head looking for a man. I talked with her after a seminar in St. Louis.

"This is a waste of time. Why do I have to learn about me? I've known who I was and what I was about for years," Ruth said bluntly. Ruth grew up in a home where she was never valued or even wanted. Her parents were always high on cocaine or drunk on vodka and paid her little attention. As a result, Ruth was tough and rugged because her life demanded it. Learning about self was an unheard of luxury.

"I raised myself," she said with a bit of pride. "If I didn't, no one else would have. Yes, I want a man in my life. I have not had good luck with men. None of those I have met really wanted to know who I was. They were flaky," she said.

Ruth was wrong. The men Ruth encountered had trouble getting to know her because she didn't know herself. Without self-knowledge, she had no basis for a relationship. Learning about self gives a queen her power. A look within gives her strength.

One of the best tools ever for evaluating your personality is the David Keirsey personality assessment test. I recommend the book *Please Understand Me II.* More than twenty years ago I read this book. I took the personality assessment it includes and finally understood why I did what I did. It changed my life. The uncertainty and insecurity that plagued me evaporated. I became confident and sure, because I knew who I was dealing with—me. What makes the assessment test so accurate is that it helps explain why you do what you do. "There is no substitute for careful and informed observation. But self-examination is quite foreign to most people, and so devices like this questionnaire can be useful in getting you started by asking questions about your preferred attitudes and actions.[1] My personality type is ENFJ, which means that I am extraverted, sensing, observant, and perceiving.

Queens not only know themselves psychologically, they are unmovable in their conviction that they have a divine destiny. Have you ever felt like you were always bumping into obstacles or hindrances as you tried to press forward? If so, this could mean that you are out of your purpose. God has a purpose for everyone. God's plans are higher and grander than ours can ever be. Before you were born, God predetermined a purpose for your life. It makes sense to tap into that purpose and walk in the pathways that God has already created for you. According to 1 Corinthians 12:7, "To each is given the manifestation of the Spirit for common good. To one is given through the Spirit the utterance of wisdom, and to another the utterance of knowledge according to the same Spirit, to another faith by the same Spirit, to another gifts of healing by the one Spirit, to another the working of miracles." These divine gifts are real and lodged inside all of us. Our task is to discover them. Mickie did.

Mickie's life took a 360-degree turn once she figured out who she was. She was a woman who reluctantly came for counseling. (I suspect that family had pressured her to come, because she sure did not want to be there.) If ever there was an aimless life floating nowhere good, it was Mickie's. At thirty-five, she had no hopes, dreams, or direction. She had three children by three different men and a truckload of apathy about her future. A directionless woman will fall for anything. Her job was at a standstill and her attitude was sullen and nasty. And she wondered why she did not have a man. Like Ruth, she was a shell of a woman.

When I told Mickie about a wonderful book titled *God's Purpose for You,* she was barely moved. It is an assessment tool that brings to the surface God's plan for us. It unlocks your spiritual gifts and helps you to put them to work for the good of the world.

Weeks later, she told me, "I bought the book not because you recommended it to me, but because I felt like something was missing inside of me. After I read it, I answered the questions in the back and I started laughing so hard. According to the book, I have the gift of wisdom. Me? Maybe they are right? Maybe I am wise?" I saw a queen in the making.

QUEENS' HOMES ARE THEIR CASTLES

Queens unleash their flavor and flare on a budget if need be. You must claim your surroundings and have dominion. If you are timid at home, you will be timid in other vital areas. Make the space yours. Do not hold back. Developing comfort with your surroundings must come before you give energy to seeking a man in your life. Where you live and how you live should never compromise your crown. Having a good feeling about where you live gives you a sense of being grounded, that you belong. It gives you roots. Whether or not it's an efficiency or a spacious house with square footage for days, make it yours.

A single woman who is too marriage-minded cannot make her home a castle because she feels she is contingent—meaning she won't be there long. Her life is lived waiting for him to come, and then she can move on to something better. This was the case with Jill. Jill was waiting on a husband before she could enjoy her ultracontemporary condominium. Her abode was loaded with the newest amenities but it was hollow. It was hollow because the living soul inside of it refused to thrive. Jill would not unpack her boxes. She refused to hang her impressive collection of artwork on the walls or to place her collection of Steuben figures on the intricate shelving sprinkled generously throughout.

Jill was locked in a state of "what if." She would not take authority over what was hers. She was afraid to allow herself permanency. Her engagement was abruptly ended because her ex-fiancé found out that she was cheating with another man. Jill ended up with neither man and is holding her breath till one of them comes back for her. "Maybe," she thought in the back in her mind," I'll get back together with Chester or George. One of them will come back and move in, and all will be well. I'm just here for the moment."

The Bible tells us, "Wisdom has built her house" (Prov. 9:1). This means feather your own nest and get comfortable. We don't know how long we'll be living solo, so live well. Kate is one such wise woman, and I find joy in her. She knows that her home is her castle and is not reluctant to be who she is. Her house is pink. "I like the color pink and pink is what my house shall be," she said. "It is feminine and frilly. Yes my future will probably include a husband some day, but I can't live my life waiting on him to come or try and predetermine what colors he will like." This is wisdom: comfort where you are, expressed in your living quarters.

Also, think of your home as your incubator. Incubators are safe, warm, cozy places that protect us. Once your surroundings are comfortable and reflect who you proudly are, it will soothe, nurture, and comfort you the way your favorite house slippers do. Where you live must be your haven and not your hell. It's your power base where you can recharge and energize yourself.

Do You Know Your Neighbors?

A comfortable dwelling place gives you the courage to learn your surroundings. Make sure that you are familiar with your geographical area. If possible, walk the streets and become familiar with the faces, homes, businesses, and the landscape. As you meet people, you are building your own social web. Familiarity creates confidence, and confidence keeps the crown on your head. In many ways, our societal fabric is shredded because we don't have neighborly connections with those around us. There is no embarrassment to meet the new neighbors as a single woman. God made you somebody all by yourself. Building positive connections with those around you is healthy and good for your self-esteem. "Unfortunately, when women are unhappy with where they live, they may blame it on the absence of a partner rather than on the incompatibility of their personality with the location—the city as well as the neighborhood—of their home." You can be happy where you live and how you live if you make it a priority.[2]

Should You Own or Should You Rent?

There is nothing wrong with renting, especially if that is what your finances or circumstances dictate. Owning what you live in, however, gives you a delightful sense of power and control. More single women are becoming homeowners.

Home ownership for a single woman makes a statement to the world about who she is. On the positive side it says, "She is in control." On the negative side it says, "She's desperate, has given up on marriage, and has resigned herself to live alone." Single women homeowners face resentment. Your family may be opposed to you buying a home because it has been said, "It will chase a man away." That's what happened to Teresa. Her elderly parents were old-fashioned. They considered home ownership something that husbands, not single women, initiated.

"My folks begged me to rent as long as I could," recalled Teresa, an elementary school teacher with a lucrative cosmetic sales job on the side. "They believed that if I owned a home, a man would not be attracted to me. They were right. I rented and stayed in my apartment for five years and it attracted men—but the wrong kind. All I met were bottom dwellers. They weren't going anywhere, had no desire to leave, and were threatened by my plans to come up," she explained. "Any man who is looking for a woman with less and can't handle a woman with more is not the man for me!"

Buying a home is a major decision. Make sure that you are ready. Here are a few questions to ask yourself:

- Are you old enough to own a house?
- Are you worthy of owning a house?
- Can you picture yourself sitting in your home?
- Can you picture how you would spend your evenings?
- Can you imagine inviting your parents/siblings/grandparents to dinner?
- What would be the best part about owning your own home?
- What is the worst part about owning your own home?[3]

Should you have a roommate? Yes, it is possible for two queens to share one roof. When two women opt to live as roommates they combine their financial resources and are poised to purchase an even larger home together. The benefits range from shared meals, emergency child care, and financial stability. Put your expectations in writing. And if need be, interview potential roommates. You only want the best.

QUEENS RADIATE IN THE WORKPLACE

You don't simply have a nine-to-five job. You are engaged in meaningful work that utilizes your personal best. You know yourself and you have positioned yourself precisely where you ought to be. You excel in the office. You put your best foot forward and move up each rung of the career ladder. If you are self-employed, you enjoy the fruits of entrepreneurship. Our careers are extensions of who we are.

Single women who are focused and pleased with their careers are not anxious about men. Why? Women who have something meaningful in their lives have a reason to smile. A great job does not replace a good man, but the job does make life full and satisfying.

Learning to aim high should be a lesson from childhood, yet this was not taught to many of us. If we intentionally or subconsciously do not invest effort to make our careers meaningful, we will suffer. Many of us cannot see ourselves as successful at work. At an early age, through gender role stereotyping, society says which occupations are suitable for girls and boys to learn. The results are limited career choices and planning. In addition, girls suffer from restricted career awareness because they lack information about nontraditional career choices, particularly those related to mathematics, science, and engineering.

As a result, some sisters don't aspire occupationally. They put on blinders that block their career possibilities. Instead, they concentrate on a man to save them. Carla had a job history that was a litany of disaster. I diagnosed her issue at a Philadelphia seminar. She was employment tumbleweed who rolled from job to job to job. She invested little of her time working and much of her time looking for a man or scheming how to get one into her life. Despite a bachelor's degree from an Ivy League college, she was not productive. Carla was sabotaging her career by focusing on a man too much.

"I'd daydream from nine to five, wondering what it would be like to meet him and walk down the aisle," she recalled. "I was young and restless. Going to work was just something I did in between bars, nights clubs, and happy hours. Even when I was in my office I was on the Internet at online dating services."

The opposite of a sister like Carla is Vivian, who is far too consumed by her job to be a queen. Getting in too deep with the job is known as workaholism. Workaholism is a symptom that something is wrong. "The danger for some women, though, is that work becomes their only source of gratification, of feeling valued. For these women, workaholism has become a substitute for real life."[4] They don't have the man so they make up for him with long hours and drastic dedication to the job. In effect, they marry the job.

When Vivian's marriage failed, she married the job. She decided to block the pain of her divorce by plunging into her law practice. This was a convenient move because the practice demanded twelve- to fourteen-hour days regularly. The firm welcomed those who put their lives on hold for the business; arrive early, eat lunch at the desk, stay late, give up weekends, and come in on holidays. She was effective and competent in her chosen profession, but what about her social life or activities outside the office?

"They were nonexistent," Vivian explained. "I did not want to come home to an empty anything. So I didn't come home. The office was my home, and my coworkers were my family. The shame from the divorce made me feel like a failure with men. I did not have any interest in trying to date. What for? That was not my skill set—clearly. It felt good to linger where I could make a difference. I knew that I was a great lawyer, but I flunked being a wife."

Now we know what a queen looks like, walks like, prays like, and lives like. How do we get there? We have twelve chapters ahead of us that will pave the way. This journey is challenging and often tedious, but worth it. Please do not grow weary. You owe it to yourself to perform this work on yourself. No one else can do it but you.

Next is the subject of personal change. It is true that only babies like to be changed, but as a queen, you must always make yourself open to and excited about change. Change means improvement, and improvement means getting better and better. Who wouldn't want that?

QUESTIONS FOR REFLECTION

1. Are you a veteran queen? If so, how long have you been at this level?
2. Are you a rookie queen? How does it feel to finally get here?
3. Are you a queen in the making? What challenges are you facing right now?
4. What will you need to do to strengthen your relationship with God?
5. How well do you know yourself? You probably need to know more. What steps will you take to learn more about you? Are you afraid of this process? Why?
6. Is your home your castle or just a holding pen until he arrives?
7. What do you need to do to make your home an incubator?
8. Are you thriving at work? Do you need to make changes there? Are you willing to make work work for you?

PRAYER

Empowering God, I know that you created me to be a queen long before the beginning of time. I receive the blessings that you have for me. I realize that I am made for a higher purpose. Unleash in me the power to be who you made me. Let me be fearless of the unknown, open to all of your possibilities, and prepared for the regal life of one of your queens. Amen.

2 · REPROGRAM YOUR MOTHERBOARD

My church's computer technician came by my office the other day to make changes on my system. I watched him work in amazement and asked, "What are you doing?" He said, "I am reprogramming your motherboard." "What's that?" I asked. He explained that the motherboard contains all the parts of the computer: the processor, the connectors, and more. If it is not programmed correctly, the computer cannot process the commands of the user.

Immediately I began to think about single women who want to be married but have motherboards (or minds) that are not programmed with positive thoughts about themselves and marriage. This flaw will prevent them from processing the commands or desires of their hearts. Queens, let's wipe the slate clean of all the negative impressions that are crammed inside you. They are like sludge that clogs the passageways of your system. They are like a fog that blurs you from seeing the real terrain. If allowed, they have the potential to shut down your ability to positively view others, including men. Rather than being a blessing to someone, you'll wind up a warped and twisted sister, too bent out of shape by rumor, innuendo, and decades-old mishaps. You'll be a pain to yourself and others. There is a better way. It's called change.

It takes a lot of courage to admit that there are erroneous thoughts that should be addressed in your life. There may be deep-seated, unspoken, tightly held thoughts plaguing you. Some of these thoughts may have been passed down through your family. Others might have been picked up from your buddies. You may feel ashamed that you harbor such thoughts, or you may feel anger that this book has touched on such personal matters. But we are queens on a journey and even the smallest bump in the road can detour and delay your ascent to the throne.

In this chapter, I seek to help you reprogram your thinking about yourself and about men. To help you, I have identified a few of the most common pieces of sludge in our motherboards. These thoughts are probably swirling around in your mind and they need to come out. They are: "all men are dogs," "marriage is easy," "marriage is the ultimate in my life and without it I am nothing," and "shacking up works." After the sludge is removed, I'll help you put positive acts in their place: a love hiatus, dating yourself, writing a love resume, reclaiming your virginity, and abstaining from sex.

"ALL MEN ARE DOGS"

This perennial put-down easily rolls off the tongues of angry, tortured sisters. Rage and disappointment have taken their world hostage and they speak the language of captive women. Saying that all men are dogs gives them a location for their blame. It is a convenient target for their frustration. Please believe me, I feel the pain. This may describe you. Relating to men can be a trying process. They can make you feel very good or make you feel very bad. How we respond to that is what makes us queens. We can rise above the negative chatter. If, however, you still feel this way, don't worry. There is help. You can overcome the anger like Jonquil did.

"I hated men," she said calmly. This thirty-two-year-old single mother of a ten-month-old child seemingly had a reason. Jonquil fell in love with Hakim, began having unprotected sex, and accidentally became pregnant. Upon learning of the pregnancy, Hakim broke up with her and was never heard from again. "To say that I hated him and all men was an understatement," she said. "I felt betrayed, lied to, and even abused. Hakim said that he loved me and I believed him. If he could so easily lie to me, I figured that no man had the capacity to be true to any woman—so why bother trusting them?"

My diagnosis was that Jonquil built walls of anger around herself and determined that no man could be trusted. "All men are dogs" was her conclusion." Jonquil's feelings soon colored her behavior. She was hostile and almost belligerent to men who simply greeted her as they passed by. If a man approached her to ask her name and attempt to request a date, she served up an ice-cold response. She'd frown, look him up and down and curtly reply, "I don't think so."

In a counseling session, I told Jonquil, "Your first step toward healing is to realize that numerically, all men cannot possibly be dogs. It is not fair to them or you to paint them with such a wide and slanderous brush. There are good men out there."

What is a dog? A dog is the term used to describe men who mistreat and abuse women in relationships. They seem to enjoy it and string along more than one woman at a time. There are church-going dogs and club-going dogs. There are old dogs and new dogs. There are dogs in the pulpit and dogs in the pews.

It may be interesting to learn the origins of this doggish, canine behavior. "There is a long tradition of churchmen behaving badly. Like their hoochie counterparts, dogs also have biblical roots. In 2 Corinthians 3:6 we learn about the forerunners of dogs: "for among them are those who enter into households and captivate weak women, weighed down with sin, led on by various impulses."[1]

Lawrence Gary agrees about dogs and concurrently writes from a more analytical perspective, "Success with women is important to many men because they are engaged in covert competition with other men. They believe that through success they will avoid ridicule and will be considered 'hip.' In the process the women become the target and the game becomes an end in itself rather than a means to an end."[2]

Another reason to refrain from calling all men dogs is that our speech is very powerful; what we say can impact our lives. "So also the tongue is a small member, yet it boasts of great exploits. How great a forest is set ablaze by a small fire" (James 3:5). It is no longer wise to make such statements. All men are not dogs. Men cannot be grouped into any single category except the male category. Admittedly, there are some men who regularly display detrimental, devious, doggish behavior toward women. But all men do not. When we make blanket statements, we come down off of our queenly perch and lower ourselves to a level where the dogs really are. Such statements cancel the faith needed for the power of God to deliver and keep us from doggish men. (See more about this topic in chapter 9.)

Let's replace this trash with the truth; there are some good men out there. Have faith and believe that decent men will come into your life. Toward this end, I constantly search for great men and showcase them in the reality television program that I created and produce called *Mission Get Married.* This is a program that takes a mess and turns him into marriage material. In the first season of the show, I presented Derrick. He was a confessed ladies' man, and with his bodybuilder/personal trainer physique, it was very believable. Across the city was a trail of broken-hearted women whom he had loved—and left. He was quite formidable. Yet Derrick wanted to be married. This desire revealed to me that he did not enjoy being a dog. He was merely caught up in a cycle or a negative way of living. He wanted a better life. Derrick was able to become a new man and leave his doggish ways behind with counseling and pastoral encouragement.

"Now I take my time to get to know a woman," Derrick said. I am not in such a rush anymore. Before, it was meet as many as I could. Now it's slow down; learn her from the inside out first."

"MARRIAGE IS EASY"

Misnomers about marriage are detrimental to the single woman who is striving toward queenliness, because she needs the truth. Whether she ever marries or not, the misinformation will pollute her and her understanding of the institution. It is best to be informed. The ignorant pay a great price in the world of queens. Ignorance influences the way a woman interacts with men and the way she carries herself. She will wind up unprepared and overwhelmed. If marriage were easy, I believe that there would be greater numbers of marriage in the African American community. There are startling statistics about the low marriage rates in the African American community. "The United States census reports that less than 50 percent of African American families are husband-wife, and 70 percent of the community's children are born outside of intact families."[3]

Here is what can happen when marriage is considered easy. Sherry cheapened marriage by believing that all one needed to do was to simply walk down the aisle of a church and live happily ever after. "Everything was supposed to happen on its own. Nobody around me was married when I was growing up. I just saw it on TV. It looked like all they did was go to work, come home, eat, and go to bed. That's not hard at all," she said. As a result, Sherry began praying for a husband without knowing what marriage was all about. This is a prime example of the need to be careful about what we pray for.

Such thoughts place us in the wrong mindset when we approach marriage and can set us up to fail. For example, Sherry's attitude in the dating scene was haphazard. She was not very selective. She thought that any man would do because once they got married, she'd change him and everything would be all right. She had not considered his temperament, his background, or his future goals. As she focused on the ease factor, she ignored the rest.

Let's replace this error with education. The institution of marriage is a sacred relationship that should be valued and revered. Marriage is an intricate dance between a man, a woman, and God. God weaves them together in a marvelously divine way. In Ephesians 5:31 we read: "For this reason a man will leave his father and mother and be joined to his wife, and the two will become one flesh. This is great mystery . . ."

Rather than a stroll through the park, marriage is more like a marathon race. The challenge of marriage is not so much planning the wedding, but planning how to blend the two lives. Jesus endorsed marriage. He was an invited guest at the wedding at Cana (John 2:1); this means that marriage was important enough of an event for him to attend.

Also vitally important to marriage is the covenant.

> The key concept in the understanding of Christian marriage is God's continuing unquestioned grace-filled love and the couple's sharing of this love with each other and others. This covenant model includes at least two basic elements. The first element is your mutual intention as partners to love and cherish each other, as God has loved you. This is your basic goal. From this comes the second; your mutual commitment to work through your relationship in love, for your own growth, for the growth of your spouse, and then together for the growth of others.[4]

"MARRIAGE THE ULTIMATE; WITHOUT IT I AM NOTHING"

This sludge is the extreme opposite of the previous statement. Like its predecessor, it too is a statement of desperation that must now be removed from your motherboard. Get the bleach and cleansers quick!! Why? Believing that you are nothing without marriage is tragically flawed. It equates your value with your marital status. It devalues your worth in your own eyes. The statement gives marriage too much power over your life. Marriage can be a goal, but not the consuming focus of your life. Queens can't let a quest for marriage crush them. This coupling off frenzy may be an issue of our society, but it does not have to be yours. How you successfully reject this will determine your happiness.

On her third divorce, Clarise lived by this motherboard mistake. So wedded to the idea that marriage is a must for survival, she is searching for husband number four. "I am a woman who has to be married," she explained. "I was made for marriage and I know that I'll find the perfect one for me. I don't do well solo." If Clarise does not reprogram herself, she will not find a solid marriage, but a repetition of marital mess.

Let's convert this counteractively with the belief that the ultimate for you is living God's purpose. We all have a divine purpose in life. That is, we were not some accident by mom and dad. God had you in mind eons ago and designed your destiny to make an impact on the world. So many women miss God's blessing of greatness in their dogged pursuit of marriage. I am not saying to give up on marriage; I am saying to give God a chance first.

Jeremiah 29:11 says, "For surely I know the plans I have for you, says the Lord, plans for your welfare and not for harm, to give you a future with hope." When a woman does not live like she believes this, she winds up with no purpose, which leads to trouble. "Purposelessness sets you up to think you have the sort of life you need to be rescued from. That "rescue me" mentality will cause you to leap for the wrong knight every time. You'll be happy he has a horse; you won't notice that his armor is looking kinda tacky and his horse is limping."[5]

"SHACKING UP WORKS"

On their motherboard, a growing number of women have the erroneous idea that "shacking up works." I am not sure where it came from. It appears to be a short cut to the altar. Cohabitating is a way of life for lots of people—in some 3.3 million households in America. According to the latest census figure, this figure is up 72 percent.[6]

Armed with this mindset, a woman settles beneath God's promise and she needs to hand in her crown. Shacking up pulls you off the throne. It is beneath you because it is a detour or a delay or even a denial of who you are. Yes, he may ultimately marry you, but at what risk to you? You know the saying, "Why buy the cow when the milk is free?" According to a study by the University of Wisconsin, should they wed, cohabitating couples exhibit poor relationship habits that prevent them from having lasting marriages. Here are four poor habits.

- They don't believe that marriage can last forever.
- They are less enthusiastic about family life.
- They do not receive the family support that married couples receive.
- They develop bad relationship habits.[7]

A caller called the radio station with this question, "My boyfriend and I have been together for ten years and lived together for eight. I've been giving him hints about marriage for years and he ignores me. We have three kids and I want them to have a legal daddy. What should I do?" I advised her, "You should move out as soon as you can and take your kids. Let God lead you to a man who will commit to you. The man you are with has grown comfortable and content with the situation. Badgering him will push him away."

Living together will not provide what you ultimately want. There is too much at risk, including your reputation, your relationship with God, and your financial issues. In some instances, cohabitating couples buy furniture, cars, and homes together. Should the relationship end, there can be difficulty recouping what you put into the relationship.

Let's replace this with the realities of commitment. In all fairness, it is not always men who shun marriage in favor of shacking up. Sometimes it is women. Vida and her live-in boyfriend Walter were well-known around the church. They were active in the choir and the singles ministry. Walter was greatly embarrassed by their "situation" as he called it. "I have asked her to marry me for years, and she refuses. I am treating her kids like they were my own. I want to make this thing legal, but she says no every time."

Vida was very direct about her lack of interest in marriage. "What is the point? We are together and we are happy. Besides I don't want to open myself to any other drama," she said.

Vida had a problem with commitment. She and thousands of other people run from it because it makes them feel vulnerable and without control. Commitment phobes have difficulty focusing on one person in a relationship and tend to move quickly from one person to another. Basically, they want control. Commitment phobes are not bad people. They are people with anxiety about being confined or controlled. The anxiety is so intense that they feel a strong urge to be free. Pressuring them will not produce the results you want. They may run as a result.

Vida felt she had control, but what she actually had was a shell of a relationship. So much more was available. To be helped, she needed to examine her life, seek changes, and move beyond her fears. A life built around fear is terrible. For others, commitment can be learned behavior. Begin with a small, short-term project. If you complete it, proceed to more obligations. Watch your self-confidence increase as you succeed.

TAKE SOME NEEDED TIME APART

Now it is time to add items to your motherboard. The first item is time for you. In order to achieve this, it may mean taking some social time away from men. No, you are not putting men down or casting them away. Nor are you becoming a nun. It is necessary to pull away and reflect on your situation free from outside distractions. Even if you haven't dated in a while, you can participate in this purposeful exercise.

Cynthia said, "I need time away from the male of the species." She was in the midst of separating from her husband and she was confused. Although technically she was still married, her hormones wanted to be back in the club shaking it up, exploring new men and adventures. Praise God, something inside of her said, "Slow down." I call it a love hiatus, which is a time out from relationships. It is a break that gives you much-needed space to reflect, realize, and realign yourself. There is power and strength to be found in self-focus. Especially if chapter 1 has been mastered.

During your love hiatus, experience the luxury of dating yourself. Why not take yourself to those places that you've always wanted to go? It could be a day trip to the history museum or a cruise to the Mediterranean. In the context of social settings, dating yourself will make you feel special. If you treat yourself well, things may be different when you reenter the dating scene. First, it may raise the bar of expectation. After dating yourself, you will have treated yourself so well that your perspective of dating will be raised. You will be at a new level and will have no need to come down. Second, there will be a decreased tolerance for mess. Bravo! We accept too much mess as it is. This decreased tolerance will limit the drama that comes into your dating world. Rather than putting up with it for months praying that it will go away, you will have the guts to nip it in the bud as soon as it rears its ugly head. Third, the love hiatus will clarify what you like and dislike about dating. This information tends to evaporate once a woman is actually out on a date because we can be too eager to please.

During your love hiatus, write a love resume. This resume will not help you get a job. It assists you in candidly looking at your past relationships. Everyone has a past. Are you using it to your benefit? The love resume constructively looks back on previous relationships with men and finds the lessons God has for you there. If you cannot find the lesson in each relationship, you are not looking hard enough. Every one of those men came your way for a purpose.

Here is a portion of Carol's love resume.

"In 2000, I dated John from June till August. We met through mutual friends. I did not really like him. I dated him because I wanted something to do during the summer months. (This taught me that I spend too much time with the wrong guys.)

"In 2001, I dated Maurice from September until January. I met him at the gym. He was a bit clingy, but I stayed with him through the New Year so I would not be lonely over the holidays. (I learned that I used up valuable time with the wrong guy again.)

"In 2002, I dated Kirk for an entire year. I really liked him, but I found out he was just using me. (I learned that I wasted a year with someone who was no good for me. I saw the sign, but chose to stay with him anyhow.)"

Carol was candid and her resume revealed an alarming pattern of using men and being used by them. She admitted that she was wasting her time in dead-end relationships. The resume reflections encouraged her to take a love hiatus to examine what she did and how she could be more selective about men and aware of her feelings in the future.

FASTING

The spiritual practice of fasting should be added to your motherboard. Fasting is commitment to voluntarily go without something that you enjoy for the glory of God. We fast to gain access to God and to submit special concerns before God. For example, when Esther prepared to make a major request before the king, she and her maids fasted first. "Go, gather all the Jews to be found in Susa, and hold a fast on my behalf, and neither eat nor drink for three days, night or day. I and my maids will also fast as you do" (Esth. 4:16). When you fast, dedicate it to a purpose that you can achieve and to what God can bless. Perhaps you will fast to achieve peace of mind about your singleness or your struggle to feel like the queen you are.

Fasting is not a mystical, intangible act. Fasting is one of the most concrete ways to connect with God and demonstrate your devotion to God. For some, going without food is the best way to fast. A fast from food is very demanding because it deprives you of a favorite pastime—eating! Sadly, when we are asked to make a choice between sacrificing for God and eating a pork chop, the pork chop may win. There are three types of food fasts. First is the *normal fast.* You consume no solid foods, only water or other liquids. Second is the *absolute fast.* You consume absolutely no solid foods or liquids. This is what Paul did after his experience on the Damascus road, as recorded in Acts 9:9. "For three days he was without sight, and neither ate nor drank." The third type of fast is the *partial fast.* It restricts certain foods. Daniel observed this in Daniel 10:2–3, "At that time I, Daniel, had been mourning for three weeks. I had eaten no rich food, no meat or wine had entered my mouth . . ."

Medical restraints keep others away from food fasts. They may benefit from fasting from other things, such as listening to the radio, watching television, reading, or talking. This means getting off the telephone and the Internet and putting away the magazines and novels. The time invested in talking or reading goes into prayer and reflection on God.

While fasting, don't put on a show. It's not a topic to be bragged about in the hair salon. And put a smile on your face. Fasting is not killing you, it is correcting you. In Matthew 6:16–18 we are directed, "And whenever you fast, do not look dismal, like the hypocrites, for they disfigure their faces so as to show others that they are fasting. Truly I tell you, they have received their reward. But when you fast, put oil on your head and wash your face so that your fasting may be seen not by others but by your Father who is in secret."

Fasting cleanses your spirit and body. The benefit of fasting is to flush out toxins in your body. Included in cleansing the body of toxins is the purging of emotional and spiritual toxins. Every one of us could use a type of spiritual enema, right? In Isaiah 58:6 we learn that fasting breaks up and destroys negatives in our lives. "Is not this the fast that I choose: to loose the bonds of injustice, to undo the thongs of the yoke, to let the oppressed go free, and to break every yoke?"

One of the best results of fasting is the inner discipline that it builds. As you increase your ability to turn away from food and turn toward God, you will be strengthened inwardly. Those internal spiritual muscles are indispensable for dealing with the struggles of life. A wonderful example of this is Jesus in the wilderness facing the temptations of the devil found in Matthew 4:3–4. He is fasting and, instead of getting weaker, he is getting strong due to the power of the Word. "The tempter came and said to him, 'If you are the Son of God, command these stones to become loaves of bread.' But he answered, 'It is written, "One does not live by bread alone, but by every word that comes from the mouth of God."'"

RECLAIM YOUR VIRGINITY

I recommend that you reclaim your virginity to completely reprogram your motherboard. If you are a virgin, I applaud you. Congratulations on remaining pure. God is very proud of you for living the Bible to its fullest.

Becoming a virgin again is a radical and wonderful way to keep the crown on your head. It is possible to allow the positive power of God to renew you in the name of Jesus. No, we are not suggesting that surgery be performed to reconstruct you physically. How we see ourselves through the eyes of faith is an awesome possibility.

This brings newness and freshness to your life. Past sexual encounters may cloud and crowd your mind. Sometimes they are controlling and seemingly will not allow you to move away from a former sexual partner. Reclaiming your virginity may just keep you from losing your mind.

"I could not even think straight," Sandy confessed. "I was either thinking about sex or getting me some sex. I mean, I had it bad. I'd be sitting in church trying to sing a hymn and thinking about whom I could hook up with after service. It got to the point I said, whoa. This is too much. I am too far from where God wants me to be."

Reclaiming your virginity is a strong move towards redeveloping your identity, focus, and even power. We sometimes lose our personal power by giving ourselves away sexually. In return, we are hurt or rejected. Under this plan, you define you—the queen that you are. You control you. This is ultimate power.

Reclaiming your virginity benefits you mentally and emotionally. The mental benefits are that you can distance yourself from a past where you had no control. If you were sexually abused, you had no control. Survivors of rape or incest can regain a sense of personal fortitude by reclaiming their virginity because it was not freely given away. This helps them to manage the mental torture of pain and suffering. Emotionally, reclaiming your virginity can release you from an arrested emotional state due to the manner in which your virginity was taken. Perhaps you became sexually active to fit in with the popular crowd or to please a guy whom you really liked. Look at your life and determine if your emotions are out of control. Reclaiming your virginity can replace anger with joy or rage with peace.

Rape and incest survivors can omit step one of the next list and replace it with, "God, I realize that I was violated." Realize that your abuse may have caused feelings of low self-esteem and may have led to promiscuity. You are not blamed for the abuse, but you can take steps to curb the resulting behavior.

Take the following steps toward reclaiming your virginity:

- Admit it was ungodly. *God, I realize that fornication is not pleasing in your sight.* "For out of the heart come evil intentions, murder, adultery, fornication, theft, false witness, slander" (Matt. 15:19).
- Confess the sin to God. *I confess that I am a fornicator.* "If we confess our sins, he who is faithful and just will forgive us our sins and cleanse us from all unrighteousness" (1 John 1:9).
- Repent from it and refrain from it. *I do repent from fornication.* "No, I tell you; but unless you repent, you will all perish as they did" (Luke 13:3)
- Embrace celibacy. *I now will live for you by dedicating my body to you.* "Or do you not know that your body is a temple of the Holy Spirit within you, which you have from God, and that you are not your own? . . . Therefore glorify God in your body" (1 Cor. 6:19–20).

Living the celibate lifestyle is possible to all believers. Yes, it is a gift from God. Paul speaks of a "gift" in 1 Corinthians 7:7 regarding his ability to live without sex. People may not be willing to talk about it, but it is being embraced.

> Celibacy is a quiet but powerful force in the world. Just because women are not talking about it, does not mean it's not going on. In a poll of national women and their sexuality, 27 percent of women say they feel so much sex is just not worth

> it. And celibacy (no intercourse) was chosen by 33 percent of single women at one time or another, for a period of at least six months after they had been sexual earlier in their lives; almost all praise it because of the chance it gives them not to be sexually involved—to take an emotional break, focus their energy on other things.[8]

Defined, celibacy is a life without sexual intercourse. Most of us have heard of nuns and priests who were celibate due to religious vows. Unlike certain religious dictates, your experience with celibacy is not a vow never to marry. It is a pledge to God to restrain (not destroy) your sexual urges until you marry. You willingly place it on God's timetable. Don't enter this lifestyle with anger at God. God is not punishing you with this. You are really being protected. Use your faith to see down the road; your life will be better. Don't try and seek shortcuts with this. Celibacy is demanding but can be a beneficial way of life. For example, some people may participate in foreplay but not sexual intercourse. This is not a form of celibacy. And, yes, oral sex and anal sex do count as sexual intercourse. Others may choose celibacy because they are between relationships and this is an easy lifestyle; but this is not a form of celibacy. Celibacy is not a means of getting revenge on a boyfriend. Nor is celibacy a reason to seek praise and adoration from friends and family. Make sure that you are being celibate for the right reasons.

If you are going to have a celibate lifestyle, you have to develop a strategy. Celibacy will not happen by itself. Monitor your actions and, if need be, rearrange a few things. Increase your prayer time; join a Bible study class; begin godly meditation; and make the decision to fast. These spiritual disciplines will give you outer power. Monitor the type of music that you listen to, the types of television programs and movies that you watch, as well as the type of books that you read. Sexual stimulation in the media can thwart your best-laid plans.

Your friends and associates will also impact your celibacy plans. If you plan on being celibate, your friends should be too—ideally. They influence you greatly. If your girlfriends talk about what man is the best lover, you are in the wrong crowd. The pressure will be too intense and you will not receive the support that you need.

In her book *Sensual Celibacy,* Donna Marie Williams urges celibate women to look at their situations in a positive light. "The bed is an important tool of sexual lovemaking, and we tend to neglect it when there is no man in our life. Make sure that you make up your bed every morning as soon as you wake up. Buy sheets in colors that make you feel romantic and alive, and textures that feel soft and silky on the skin (satin and Egyptian cottons are wonderful)."[9]

In this chapter, I have given you the tools to reprogram your motherboard. If you are serious about being a queen, get on board with this program. The way you process crucial information probably needs to be tweaked. I pray that you press the delete button on harmful thoughts like "all men are dogs," "marriage is easy," "marriage is the ultimate in my life and without it I am nothing," and "shacking up works." I also am praying that you added positive acts like going on a love hiatus, dating yourself, writing a love resume, reclaiming your virginity, and abstaining from sex.

Now you should be reprogrammed and ready to roll on to the next challenge of getting your surroundings together!

QUESTIONS FOR REFLECTION

1. What area of your motherboard needs to be reprogrammed the most?
2. What area of your motherboard needs to be reprogrammed the least?
3. Are all men dogs in your opinion? Why or why not?
4. Have you ever considered cohabitating?
5. How will a love hiatus benefit you?

6. How will fasting benefit you?
7. Can you reclaim your virginity? What are the benefits?
8. Is celibacy a possibility for you? What will you need to change?

PRAYER

Understanding God, I need your power to help me get rid of negative ideas. They are holding me back from your glory. Please give me divine cleansing. I am inviting you to sweep them out of my mind and pour your Holy Spirit into my situation. I want to begin a love hiatus. I want to learn from my past relationships. I want to fast. I want to reclaim my virginity. I want to abstain from sex. Please help me to do all of this and more in your name. Amen.

3 · SANITIZE YOUR SITUATION

Shanda had the nerve to want a new man in her life even though she was still in relationship with four other men who ranged in various shapes and sizes. These men were leftovers and carry-overs from as far back as her high school days, twenty-five years ago. Old worn-out relationships that she could not and would not let go still lived in her heart and her head. It would be impossible to bring in someone new. There was no room and no need to. She was already full!

Even though Shanda developed a taste for leftovers, you as a queen cannot. Leftovers are remnants. They are bland, tasteless, and offensive to our palate. Some women will argue that it is all that they have so they will hold on to it. At least they have that. I gently counter: if left on the shelf of your life too long, the leftovers become sour, tainted, or even poisonous.

Leftovers cause relationships with people, places, and things to become venomous and toxic predicaments. Specifically, they can make you sick. For example, the stress of dealing with a leftover man may lower your immune system. Anger from your toxic relatives may cause ulcers. Queens have a zero tolerance policy to toxicity. We sometimes enter bad situations unaware of the potential for harm, or unfortunately we are addicted to them. This chapter will teach you how to sanitize your situation. It is a lengthy and detailed, yet needed, process. Here are the steps: recognize poisonous people, move them out of your life, erect boundaries, replace negative relationships with positive ones, sanitize your separations (if you are still married), make peace with your parents and your siblings, and repair relationships with your children.

The first tool that you will need is the ability to identify the poison. For some, it may not be easy because the poison is all that they know. They cut their teeth on nonstop chaos. They were reared in such homes. Michelle enjoys describing herself as a drama queen, but the truth is, she was reared in a drama home and she is merely reflecting what she was taught by her parents. Growing up, Michelle learned how to converse by screaming. Tension was a normal feeling and deep mistrust and anger were everyday emotions. "Didn't everyone grow up like this?" she asked. Her life is a toxic dump because she is surrounded by people who are not good for her. Michelle could not change until she knew the difference between healthy and unhealthy ways to communicate.

Got poison in your life? Here is a simple way to identify poisonous persons or predicaments. First, they make you feel unsafe, uncomfortable, or ill at ease. Second, poisonous predicaments put a strange feeling in the pit of your stomach that you can't identify. Listen to your inner self. Trust your own instincts. Don't be naïve. There are people who intend to harm you. They are malicious, vicious, and mean. Their poison is planned and premeditated. Your duty is to protect yourself.

Michael Moore, author of *Coping With Toxic People,* provides a more detailed look at this:

TOXIC PEOPLE

- rob us of our dignity
- destroy our self-confidence
- increase our stress levels

- destroy our morale
- erode our self-esteem
- foster negativity
- decrease productivity
- make life hellish
- are abusive
- are toxic because they can get away with it and it works for them[1]

Moore offers a strategy for dealing with them. Remember that you can't change toxic people, but you can learn to cope with them. Here are some effective strategies that you can try:

- Always stand at eye level with the person you are confronting. Never have them standing over you looking down.
- Respect the toxic person and always expect respect in return. Settle for nothing less.
- Remain calm.
- Listen attentively.
- Don't argue or interrupt, just listen.
- Don't accuse or judge, just state how you feel.
- If the toxic person tries to verbally bully you, just say, "I don't allow people to treat me this way." Then slowly and calmly walk away.[2]

Don't label every relationship that went bad as poisonous. The relationship simply may have been a mistake or maybe it was not meant to last. There are some relationships that should be kept and some should be discarded. This is a skill-set that queens must develop. It is a mark of maturity to be able to distinguish between a friend and a person who is around for convenience—namely theirs. This is sanitizing your situation. It is cleaning out the germy leftovers of your life. You may have formed an attachment to them or an infestation from them has developed inside you. Either way it's got to go. Here's how you can determine what goes and what stays.

GOES	STAYS
hurts you	helps you
harasses you	encourages you
produces guilt	produces joy
opens wounds	no scars are produced
tears you down	builds you up

BOUNDARIES ARE A MUST

Why is it so hard to let go of the relationships that are obviously negative? It is all about the boundaries. The way we feel about ourselves helps determine the way we view our choices. The degree to which we tolerate the good or bad determines our level of self-esteem. This is a critical issue for single women in particular. I wish we were taught about our boundaries back in kindergarten, along with our colors, numbers, and ABCs. Our lives and relationships would be better. For example, if you accept poor treatment from a man you are dating because you feel that you can't do any better, then you have boundary issues. Or if the women at church talk about you and put you down, yet you choose to spend time with them anyway, you have boundary issues. An alarmingly poor level of self-esteem keeps you in a relationship that you do not need. Erect boundaries immediately. Protect your boundaries at all costs.

Take your hands and draw a line in the air all around your body. You are defining the area that you are responsible for. This is your boundary. There are physical boundaries, emotional boundaries, psychological and sexual boundaries, and they belong to you. You control them. You must. We can only control ourselves and what happens in our space. We cannot control others. The purpose of setting boundaries is to take care of you. It is a part of respecting yourself and showing others that they must respect you too. Boundaries help you define yourself. We need to continually define who we are in the presence of other people as well as during times alone. Boundaries inform others and self of what is acceptable and unacceptable treatment. We must also be prepared to protect our boundaries after we set them.

Without boundaries, we are prone to blindly follow, link with others, and enter relationships with people who do not have boundaries and/or will not respect ours. Without boundaries, we run the risk of losing our identity, never knowing who we are, never feeling good enough, and harboring a responsibility for the happiness of others.

I met a young woman with severe boundary issues as she was being expelled from the university she was attending. Tina had been arrested by the campus police for destroying the property of her ex-boyfriend. "We kept breaking up and getting back together," she said. "I felt like he was my man. He said he was. So why was he in another woman's room? I had to teach him a lesson." This is a boundary issue because Tina did not understand that her anger did not give her permission to hurt her boyfriend.

According to police reports, Tina's ex-boyfriend had filed dozens of complaints that she was stalking him. They had been high school sweethearts but had broken up during the senior year. She decided to follow him to college even though the relationship was over. Tina used her mother's credit cards and her dad's car to woo him back. Their reunions were short-lived and her violent streak emerged every time. As I talked with her, the campus police and local police were escorting her and her belongings out of the city. Tina's boundaries were nonexistent. If she'd had some back in high school, she would have been able to let the ex-boyfriend go. All she ended up with was a police record, a sexually transmitted disease, and no college education.

Queen, boundaries are not optional. Accepting this fact is a major step toward sanitizing your situations. The ability to end negative relationships is a boundary issue. We sometimes don't have strength to say "enough" to a negative person. Putting someone out of our lives seems impossible because we feel guilty about hurting that person's feelings. It is of little consequence that our feelings are being trampled when we place the other person's feelings above our own. That person's feelings dictate our actions. Someone else controls us. We don't want to disappoint. We feel guilt because we've been socialized to make everybody happy, to keep the party going, to keep a smile on everyone's face. You can stop the madness now.

The madness is based on the inability to say "no." Our world is filled with what I call "yes" women. These are women who are unable to stand up for themselves. They say "yes" in situations in which they'd rather say "no." Saying "yes" instead of "no" is a futile attempt to cling to others. Uttering the word "no" would erect a boundary that would separate us from others, and this is what is so frightening. Saying "yes" means we will have to stand alone. I know a lot about this because I am a reformed "yes" woman. I dreaded saying "no" to anyone. I only learned to say "no" after I reached my mid-thirties. Prior to that time, I was uncomfortable and unable to say "no." I thought it might cause people to dislike me, or it might cast me in an unfavorable light. I said "yes" because if I spoke up, maybe they would not like me. Being liked and feeling a part of the group was most important. I was content to get along by a destructive means—sacrificing myself.

The first year that I was a senior pastor of a church, I finally found the courage to say "no." Many of the congregants treated me shabbily as their new pastor. (Typical treatment for a "yes" woman.) They ran over me and disrespected me. I shall never forget the day that I said "no." I remember what I was wearing, what the weather was like, and how I had styled my hair. Actually the situation that I was dealing with had gotten on my last good nerve. I was at my breaking point. We were in a church business meeting and some of the more menacing leaders were pushing me in a direction that I knew I did not need to go. I had previously acquiesced to their requests in typical "yes" woman compliance. But not this time. I suddenly grew a backbone and I refused to bow down! I said "no," and it felt good. I said it again, and realized that the sun was still in the sky. I said "no" a third time—for the Holy Ghost. It was a religious experience of liberation and connecting with God! Maybe today is your day to say "no!"

CLOSURE IS A GOOD THING

The ability to end a poisonous predicament is a mark of a queen. Bringing a negative encounter to a conclusion should be joyous. Waking up from a bad dream is good. Closure is our way of waking up and ending the nighttime terror. We erroneously see closure as a failure, but it is a success.

Think about your relationships and determine the ones that cry out for closure. These are the loose strings and dangling people who do us no good. They may be left over from your childhood, or even your marriage—problems that have dangled for decades. It's not about being condemning; it's about being convinced that you have worth. It is not about you putting someone else down; it is you putting self first. It is akin to going to battle with your past for the benefit of your future. You will need strength for this, and God is able.

DISPOSE OF TRIFLING FRIENDS

Some of your friends have got to go. Questionable companions beg to be released. Friends make us or break us. Poor character corrupts the soul.

Some of them are not queens and they threaten your stay on the throne. Sanitizing your situation may cause people to think that you are better than them. The truth is, you just may think more of yourself than they think of themselves—and that's no crime. There are a host of reasons why some of your friendships with other women and even platonic relationships with men need to end. Most of us grew up with or went to school with or served in the armed services with someone we have outgrown and need to let go of. Think back; there was a friend in junior high school that demanded that you only be friends with her. Do you remember her? She'd get mad if you sat with other girls at lunch. I struggled with a childhood friend who lacked self-definition and as a result she imitated every move I made, including my hairstyles, clothes, and even school selection.

People need to be released if they betray you, reveal confidences, or attempt to control you. Before you release them, be aware of the risks. They may reveal secrets that you shared or may retaliate in other painful ways if the relationship is severed.

How do you know if you should let someone go? Ask yourself these questions. Is this someone you are ashamed of? Do you trust this person? Does he or she keep your secrets? Are the two of you highly competitive? Do you gossip about one another? Has she or he borrowed things and never returned them?

Yes, you and Boquetha have been friends since the fourth grade, but her lying, conniving ways have gotten you in trouble constantly. Weren't you almost arrested with her when the police pulled the two of you over and discovered the stolen goods in her car trunk? Weren't you almost shot when the pregnant wife of her married boyfriend opened fire? Well, be her friend from a distance, pray for her, but do not continue to spend your time with her. You are going in opposite directions. As a queen you are going up while she is going down. Remember your boundaries. You can't control her inappropriate behavior, but it can impact and infect your appropriate behavior. It can poison your queenliness.

Holding on to trifling friends is really a form of sabotage. Self-sabotage occurs when we do things subconsciously that we know will kill our chances of improvement. Shelia is sabotaging herself. She drives forty-five minutes across town to her best buddy's house to smoke weed. "None of my coworkers or neighbors are into this, so I have to go back to my roots," she said. Shelia is actually sabotaging her career. She knows that random drug testing takes place in her office. Why does she do it? Her need to feel accepted outpaces her need to succeed in life. Success can be frightening. It's a place some have never been before. She knows that she can apply for a promotion, earn more, supervise more people, make her family proud, but her trips to the other side of town shackle her to living beneath the potential that God has for her.

Here are affirmations that reinforce your decision to end a friendship.

- I am ending this friendship because it is in my best interest, and I have to put myself first, before all others, including this friend.
- I will not gossip about my friend or about our failed relationship.
- I will respect my friend's secrets and privacy after the friendship ends, just as I expect my friend to respect mine.
- I will give myself time to grieve and mourn this failed friendship, just as I would grieve or mourn the ending of any intimate relationships that I once treasured and valued.
- I am entitled to have upbeat, positive, and trustworthy friendships.[3]

Move Out Former Flames

It is also a good thing to sanitize your situations with former boyfriends. Sometimes they have the tendency to linger on longer than they should. We encourage it by not ending the relationship, failing to tie up loose ends, or being reluctant to articulate how we really feel. A woman with a lot of loose ends is often chaotic and frazzled because of the numerous unclear and muddled relationships. She is always guessing and fumbling. Living an unclear and uncertain life is more time consuming than we realize.

From their lingering status, former flames take up space in your life. Lingering means they no longer have a purpose in your life. They just hang on, like those little pills on worn parts of a sweater. They do not contribute to your improvement. They represent broken hopes and dreams. The attachment is one of convenience, usually sexual in nature.

"He just won't go away," Nita moaned. He was her ex. They had dated for six months. Things got intimate fast and within weeks, he had a key to her apartment and moved in. "He comes and goes like he owns the place. I can't stand this," she said. He still has a key because she will not demand that he return it or change the locks. "I don't want to seem mean," she explained. Nita's misdirected concern is for a homeless, jobless man who has moved into her home against her wishes.

I've discovered that sex is like cement because it creates what is called *soul ties.* Biblically, sex between unmarried persons creates *soul ties.* In Genesis 34:1–27 we find the sad saga of what can happen when sex occurs outside of marriage. Dinah and Sheckem were sexually intimate. Even though the event took place through date rape, verse three tells us "he loved the girl, and spoke tenderly to her" and "his soul was drawn to Dinah." This means that their souls were connected as a result of having been sexually intimate.

Fornication produces soul ties. Soul ties exist between people who have been sexual partners. They are bound to each other, whether they know it or not. The connection is usually subconscious and we don't realize why we can't seem to let go of the man who never treated us right. Or we can't say no to the guy who was dating several other women—plus us. You don't have to live like this.

Soul ties are problematic because they produce nonproductive guilt. Yes, God wants us to regret the fornication, but extreme guilt can be crippling. Second, soul ties cloud our ability to clearly interact with the opposite sex, forcing us into patterns of unhealthy, unproductive relationships. At a single women's retreat I talked about soul ties and the room became still and quiet. The reality that a lot of the women were tied to men scattered all over creation hit them hard. No one moved or spoke for a few minutes, that seemed even longer. Finally, one woman raised her hand and asked, "Is there anything that we can do about this?"

Severing soul ties is a spiritual sanitizing. Pray, confess, and ask God to cleanse your inner soul. Pray this prayer: "Cleansing God, I need you to sanitize my spiritual house. Please remove the soul ties from my soul. Forgive me of the sin of fornication. Restore me to me inwardly. Purge me with hyssop and I shall be clean. I desire inner cleaning that only you can provide. Amen."

SANITIZE YOUR SEPARATION

Separations occur when married couples experience difficulty and decide to spend time apart to determine if the marriage should continue. Statistics indicate that "80 percent of all married couples separate for at least two months."[4] These can be positive, healthy times of reflection or they can be destructive times of pain and suffering. Either way separations need to be sanitized. Far too often they become contaminated because they are not handled and stored properly. Married couples get comfortable sitting on the fence of indifference and they do nothing, which makes the situation even grimier. Sanitizing your separated situation takes special care. Major decisions have to be made.

A wounded/damaged marriage needs immediate medical attention. If it festers like an infected limb that gets no attention, gangrene can set in and may require amputation. If you are separated from your husband for more than six months, take action. It seems easier to sit in neutral than to move in any direction. Don't get comfortable staying separated. African Americans have high rates of separation. Decide to reconcile or divorce. Ask yourself these questions: Am I being taken advantage of? If there is infidelity, is it isolated or serial? Is the marriage worth saving? Use the famous Ann Landers question, "Are you better off with him or without him?"[5] Visit a pastor or counselor with your spouse and determine if you will remain married or not. Decide on a course of action. Inaction is toxic.

If the marriage can be saved, save it. Reconciliation requires that both you and your spouse spend quality time alone. Fragmented phone calls and hasty visits will not allow the time alone that you and he need. You and your spouse must recommit to the marriage. I recommend pastoral counseling to address those tough issues that caused the split in the first place. Good counseling can chart a pathway that gives couples the chance to survive. There is always hope for your marriage, even if you do experience a separation. One study showed that "18 percent of all couples that divorce remarry each other."[6]

Television court Judge Mablean Ephriam explained that she is divorced because her husband committed adultery. She reflected on how a woman should decide whether or not to try and save the marriage. "She should ask, have I done everything I can do? Have I been the best that I can be? Have I given my all? If she answers yes, then there is nothing more she can do. If she can't, she should get busy. As women, we let the little things cause us to complain and argue. Sometimes we need to just step back and look at the big picture."[7] If the marriage cannot be saved, let it go. Holding on to a dead relationship is not healthy on many levels. Physically, it's like carrying a cadaver. The sheer weight of the dead relationship on your back is overwhelming. Mourn the loss, but let it go. Separations tend to weigh down the spirit and keep it locked in the past, held back from other things that God has for you. Do not allow the separation to last eternally. Make decisions and move on with your life.

Do you have a fear of being divorced? Divorce has stigma, shame, and embarrassment attached to it. Don't let the fear keep you in a bad and meaningless relationship. If you decide to end the marriage, resist the urge to second-guess yourself or emotionally beat yourself up with mistakes you made. Much of the negativity surrounding divorce comes from interpretations of Jesus' comments on divorce found in Matthew 5:31–32, where he said: "'Whoever divorces his wife, let him give her a certificate of divorce.' But I say to you that anyone who divorces his wife, except on the ground of unchastity, causes her to commit adultery; and whoever marries a divorced woman commits adultery."

For generations, women have felt forced to remain in painful relationships because they feared the public wrath regarding divorce. It was more painful to get divorced and be labeled an adulteress than to stay in the mangled marriage. In Jesus' day divorce was as common as today. Divorces were facilitated by the priests and could occur for any reasons. I believe that what Jesus was saying is that divorce is a negative, and that it is best to remain married if possible. Yet the same Jesus who forgives murderers and thieves can forgive a divorcee.

It can also be noted that

> when a married couple is estranged beyond reconciliation, even after thoughtful consideration and counsel, divorce is a regrettable alternative in the midst of brokenness. It is recommended that methods of mediation be used to minimize the adversarial nature and fault-finding that are often part of our current judicial process. . . . Divorce does not preclude a new marriage. We encourage an intentional commitment of the Church and society to minister compassionately to those in the process of divorce, as well as members of divorced and remarried families, in a community of faith where God's grace is shared by all."[8]

Here is one woman's encouraging story of deciding to end her marriage despite the pain of divorce. Micki had a fabulous marriage to Carl who earned millions on and off the basketball court. They lived the lifestyle that most of us dream of: a mansion with a staff of servants, private jet, couture clothing, and more. Alas, the trappings of success did not rub off on the marriage. Carl kept women on the side. Micki thought she could enjoy the cash and ignore the affairs. She was wrong. After seven years of marriage she wanted out, but how could she leave it all behind? During her separation she came to me for counseling. I discovered her to be one of the most amazing women I've ever counseled. Micki laid out a methodical plan to sanitize her life. It was not enough to realize her marriage was poisonous. She initiated a separation, went through counseling with me, and enrolled in a divorce recovery class too. She put a support system in place to ensure her mental and emotional safety.

"I miss my life," she said mournfully. Her posh life had been pared down to a simple condo. Gone were the servants and private jets. Sister girl had to work a nine-to-five job. "Even though I am hurting, I will go through with the divorce," she said. Micki had pushed beyond the pain of losing him to set her mind on restoring herself. Months later Micki shared that upon receiving her divorce decree she began the healing process. "I returned to the site of our honeymoon—Maui. I went alone because I had to face that place or it would haunt me forever. I feel like I conquered my past and now I can move on. I prayed and I cried but I got through it. The people on the beach thought I was a crazy woman, sitting there alone, crying and praying. I may have been a crazy woman when I first got there, but when it was over, I got up as a woman with all her faculties." Micki sanitized her situation even though it hurt.

The life of a queen is balanced. As you rid yourself of negative relationships, you must replace them with positive ones. The abundance of negatives may have prevented positive ones. These include making peace with your parents and resolving sibling rivalry.

MAKING PEACE WITH PARENTS

Toxic situations exist in our families. Home is where the hurt is for a lot of people. No one is entitled to hurt you, not even a member of your own family. Sometimes this concept is difficult to comprehend if all you know is pain from your parents. Sanitizing your situation is making efforts to repair or clean up your family tree.

If you feel less than or lacking as a person, there may be the proclivity to blame your parents. Our self-concept was formed during childhood. Our parents more than likely played a major role in shaping who we are. But parental blame only goes so far. Maybe you stutter to this day because your momma yelled at you a lot. Maybe you fear men will abandon you if you fall in love with them because your daddy did. Even if your parents were not the best parents, their faults do not have to be yours. Free yourself.

Here is a story that always amazes me. There were two sisters who grew up in horrible conditions. Their parents were alcoholics who rarely gave the girls much attention, supervision, or affection. The girls practically had to raise themselves. One sister grew up and developed a drug addiction, never finished high school, and has had many failed marriages. The other sister is the CEO of her own company, a college graduate, and happily married. Both were asked the same question, "How do you explain where you are in life?" They both said, "With parents like ours what do you expect?" These sisters show us that it is possible to rise above our parents or sink to their level. The choice is ours.

The tendency to blame our mothers for the mess in our lives is more common than you may know. "Mother blaming is interwoven throughout our daily lives. At every level of conversation and discussion, in every conceivable arena, mothers are ignored, demeaned and scapegoated in jokes."[9]

Keisha's mom worked all the time to support her and the six other kids. Although she had a roof over her head and food to eat, Keisha resented her mom's time away at work. "My mother was not there for me. I had to raise myself. I avoid her today because of that and I am sure she's the reason that I am still single." Keisha was held captive by her resentment of her mother. The resentment caused her to be surly and difficult in general. In relationships she felt slighted automatically.

The essential foundation for improving our mother-daughter relationships is a thorough understanding of mother blaming, "for only when we see how easy blaming Mother is will we have a chance of doing otherwise. Only when we see the pollution can we clear the air."[10] It's never too late to relate to mom. Going back and clearing the air with her may be just what you need to move ahead. I helped Keisha to see that her mom was doing the best that she could. Survival was primary for her. She did not have the luxury of giving love, time, and conversation.

In order to mend the relationship, find qualities to respect in your mother, consider your mother's struggles, and humanize your image of your mother. Learn from her mistakes and pledge not to repeat them in your life.[11]

Another form of parental prison is anger at fathers. For millions of African American women the absence of their fathers has marred them. It literally threatens the crowns on their heads. How they handle this void is essential. "The fatherless woman is a fireball of fear.

She fears rejection. She fears abandonment. She fears commitment. The questions repeatedly posed in her mind in any situation, but most especially in male/female encounters, are these: If I extend myself, will I be accepted; will I be rejected? Because a fatherless woman knows the pain of being left, of being told implicitly that she is not wanted, she both repels and attracts relationships and circumstances where she is liable to duplicate that experience."[12]

Fatherlessness is extremely common in the African American community. One caller to the radio show asked, "I never knew my dad growing up and then he wanted to come back into my life. I let him in. When he first visited me I was so happy. But then he started showing me that he wasn't about anything. He started to do all the things my mom said he did. But the difference was that now he was doing them to me. What should I do?"

I responded, "No one has the right to hurt you, even a family member. If relating to him hurts, that means it is a toxic relationship. End it now. His patterns of abuse have emerged. You can clearly see what is happening. You have the choice of being a victim or a volunteer. Keep him at a distance. Be polite, but firm."

As the caller showed us, repairing a breach with a father can be tricky, but it is often worth the effort. If you are estranged from your father and seek communication with him, reach out to him. Be assertive and try the mail, telephone, Internet, friends, and relatives. Your efforts may be fruitful, and if not, you will be at peace knowing that you tried.

RESOLVE SIBLING RIVALRY

One big happy family? I don't think so. Getting along with brothers and sisters is not always easy. A preoccupation with sibling hatred gets in the way of being a queen. Let's say you and your sister never got along. She was always tattling to mom or spreading the secrets she read from your diary. Or you and your brother always fought. The coldness never warmed up even as adults. Some siblings are hard to love. They can be extraordinarily selfish, have an extreme sense of entitlement, be con artists, be people who need to be adored, or be people who use people."[13]

A caller to the radio show wanted to know how she could handle her sister. "She is driving me crazy. She is the baby of the family and thinks that everything should revolve around her. That stuff worked when we were kids, but we are grown now and I don't play that." I responded, "That was then; this is now. Can you forgive? You should make peace and forgive for your sake and for the family's sake."

Despite all that siblings may have done wrong, take a look at yourself. How have you acted in the family? Have you been supportive, helpful, and a team player? "It is all too easy to be swept up by a culture of blame in which we are quick to notice our siblings' shortcomings and slow to recognize their contributions and accomplishments, if we notice them at all."[14]

Forgiveness, acceptance, and tolerance can lead us to positive relationships with our siblings. We can outgrow childhood spats. Harmony with siblings is especially needed to support aging parents. The possibility of serious illness is real. If the siblings are in communication, it will be easier to make difficult health-care decisions. It's been said that a medical crisis amplifies all other family problems. You will have to make life and death decisions.

Troubles rise when someone gets sick. The Jackson family illustrates the disharmony among siblings that can occur. The sibling rivalry of the two brothers and one sister is still strong, even though they are adults. Their childhood wounds are still stinging from back in the day, but their momma is critically ill and this is the wrong time and the wrong place for family drama. Sadly, momma's illness aggravates an already bad situation, and if the siblings are not careful they may hurt momma even more with their foolishness.

Imagine the three adults huddled together in the hallway of the intensive care unit of a hospital. Inside the adjacent room their mother lies in a vegetative state due to a sudden traumatic medical crisis. The doctors say that she has no chance of recovery or restoration on this side of heaven. She is being kept alive by a machine.

Momma's emergency has brought her kids back together geographically but not emotionally.

Momma raised them single-handedly. Their dad never was in the picture, so momma's care is their responsibility. Once they grew up each sibling moved as far away from the others as possible and never looked back. They rarely kept in touch, but now momma is laying on that hospital bed, and an uneasy alliance is forced.

They squabble due to a host of family dysfunctions. The younger son runs from crisis and responsibility. The middle daughter feels compelled to keep the peace, and the older son is overbearing and controlling. They have an agonizing decision to make; what are we going to do about Momma? Their mother did not provide them with her written instructions about life support and critical medical treatment in times like these. None of the children know what she would want to happen. The burden of deciding rests on their shoulders.

The doctor asks, "What is the family's wishes regarding your mother?" Ted, forty-five, Greg, twenty-nine, and Marcia, thirty-one, now grapple with the choices.

Greg: "I can't even have this conversation. I love my mother too much." He walks away and exits the hospital.

Marcia: "I believe that momma would not want to live like this. She would trust us to do what is best, and the best thing is to release her. Now. Let's take her off the life-support system."

Ted: "No way! Girl, have you lost your mind? That's my mother you are talking about killing. She wants to live, and I hate you for not even trying to keep her alive."

Such a scenario may occur in your life. We never know what our future holds. The wise person prepares for the unexpected. Make peace in your family before the crisis hits. Forgive, end grudges, tolerate each other's differences, and strive to get along. Family unity is the key to enduring difficult times. "Now I appeal to you, brothers and sisters, by the name of our Lord Jesus Christ, that all of you be in agreement, and that there be no divisions among you, but that you be united in the same mind and the same purpose" (1 Cor. 1:10).

REPAIR RELATIONSHIPS WITH CHILDREN

It is a sad situation to be estranged from your children. Repairing the breech may mean owning up to what you did wrong as a mom or accepting what they have done. The Bible presents numerous images of mothers. Some were role models; some were lacking in maternal skills. One of the undesirable mothers was Rebekah, the mother of twin boys Jacob and Esau, found in Genesis 25:23. Rebekah loved Jacob more than Esau and she conspired with him to steal Esau's birthright. "So he went and got them and brought them to his mother; and his mother prepared savory food, such as his father loved. Then Rebekah took the best garments of her elder son Esau, which were with her in the house, and put them on her younger son Jacob; and she put the skins of the kids on his hands and on the smooth part of his neck" (Gen. 27:14–16).

Think back for a moment. Were there reasons you could not be the mother that you should have been? Was it because no one parented you? Were you caught up in your youthful mistakes and ashamed? Did you have a good mom? Have you been beating yourself up over this for years? If so, admit it and ask your children for forgiveness.

Renee's mom raised her two kids because Renee was a kid herself when she had them. "I was in high school and did not have my mothering mind in place," she reflected. "It was all about parties and boys. I let my sons fall into my mom's lap, so I could do my thing. They called me Renee and my mother was their mom. I did not know any better, but now I do. The boys see my mother as their real mother. I am just a sister to them. Is it too late for me?"

Like Renee and all other moms who are struggling, it is never too late to be a mom. A good place to begin is with our understanding of what parenting is. Our kids have enough friends; they need a parent. Sometimes our children simply do not need another pair of sneakers or a sports jersey; they need to be parented. Maybe it's time to go back to school and refresh yourself regarding what it means to be a parent.

There are three parenting styles.

Authoritarian: Parents who use this style demand strict obedience to the rules they set. Such parents are generally not responsive to a child's feelings and viewpoints. Authoritarian parents insist that things be done their way—essentially because they say so. This kind of parent tends to discourage discussion and negotiation, and takes a hard line on infractions.

Authoritative: Mothers and fathers who use this style are more democratic in their childrearing. They set the basic rules, but are willing to listen to the viewpoints of children, and revise the rules in particular situations. Authoritative parents are willing to explain their rules, and are interested in helping children understand the reasons behind those rules.

Permissive: Parents who use this style create a relatively loose environment, with few rules. Demands and punishments are often spotty and inconsistent. Outsiders who walk into the home of a family with overly permissive parents may be moved to ask: "Who's really in charge here?"[15]

Queens do not live in filthy situations. It is never too late to be the mom you wish you had been. If you have the potential to be a super mom—go for it. Perhaps you can be the type of mom found in Proverbs 31. She is exalted because of all that she does for her family and the community. "She seeks wool and flax, and works with willing hands. She is like ships of the merchant, she brings food from far away. She rises while it is still night and provides food for her household" (Prov. 31:13–15). Proof of her effectiveness can be summed up in the words: "Her children rise up and call her happy" (verse 28). Make this your goal.

Sanitizing our situations is not an option. Nor is it for the fainthearted. It requires tremendous work, but there are tremendous rewards. In this chapter we have examined the need to sanitize your situation and given you the tools to do so. Those tools were to recognize poisonous people, move them out of your life, erect boundaries, replace negative relationships with positive ones, sanitize your separations, make peace with your parents and your siblings, and repair relationships with your children.

Now you are ready to move further along in the queen regime. The next stop is revising your reason for marriage.

QUESTIONS FOR REFLECTION

1. Where is there toxicity in your life?
2. Do you have boundaries?
3. Can you identify the people who need to be put out of your life?
4. Are there relationships that cry out for closure? Why haven't you closed them?
5. Can you say no?
6. What areas of your life need a peacemaker? Your parents, children, siblings?

PRAYER

Cleansing God, I am calling on the power of heaven to sanitize my situation. God, you know of all the toxic people and predicaments that I face, and you also know how to lead me out of them. Please take my hand and lead me. Amen.

4 · REVISE YOUR REASONS

Single women have wrestled with the issue of wanting to be married since the beginning of time. We believe we know when it is the right time, but truthfully, God provides us with a season for marriage. It's about being on God's timetable. Our job is to get on God's schedule and trust in God. Before we go any further, let's stop and take an honest look at the reasons you want to be married. When I was a little girl, I would sit around with my little girlfriends and we would plan our weddings. "I'm wearing blue," I said. "I'm wearing yellow," another would say. We were all unashamedly enamored with the idea of getting married because of the fabulous weddings we planned. What are your reasons?

It is a positive desire to want marriage—especially if you've survived a host of negative experiences in the relationship department. It means that we still have hope. Otherwise, we adopt the "I don't need a man" attitude. This is when the hands-on-hips, fierce neck-working stance comes out in us after a man has left us angry beyond words. We have all felt this after a disappointment or a letdown. As a result, we decided to strike out on life alone; determined not to be hurt again. The, "I don't need a man" attitude, however, can backfire and make us crave what we despise.

Queen, I don't want you to become obsessed about marriage. It can lead to awful circumstances such as fixations on a man who does not know that you are alive. These fixations may cause you to begin the stalking phase. This is the beginning of the daily drive-bys past his house just to get a glimpse of him. Here is what differentiates an obsession from a want. Obsessions drive and haunt you. Wants are controllable desires. Obsessions cause feelings of inferiority if the object is not obtained. Wants are realistic and have limits. It is abnormal to fixate over marriage. It is normal to want to be in a marriage. Most of us were wired to seek marriage. We were created by God to desire close relationships that can lead to marriage. Never let anyone make you feel ashamed of the want for marriage. That's not the point of this chapter. If you want to marry, I want you to also.

Obsessions will lead to messy lives. We wind up giving away the store before there is even an interest in purchasing the goods. We cook, clean, shop, and pamper a man in hopes of landing and holding on to him. In extreme cases, we attempt to buy his love with purchases of designer suits, cars, homes, and lavish vacations.

Audrey Chapman, the noted relationship expert, says, "Obsessing about finding a man is debilitating because it keeps women focused on the wrong issues. What they need to focus on is how to take better care of themselves, ask for support from others, and make better choices about the men in their lives."[1]

This chapter will help you examine the reasons why you want to get married. Motivations are important because they are the foundation of all that we do. There are five areas fueled by obsession: family pressure, jealousy of married women, the fear of being alone, your biological clock ticking, and/or being out of control sexually. These are negative reasons that need to be revised. I have also identified five sound reasons to want a man. These are what I called "controlled wants." They won't drive you anywhere; you can stop and start them on your schedule. They are as follows: you have a happy self, you have a healthy understanding of men, you have healed from your relationship wounds, your singleness is together, and you love yourself.

FAMILY PRESSURE

Family pressure is like a virtual pressure cooker. The compression force does not stop. It comes from all sides with the purpose of reducing you to mush. Family members have access to us like no one else. They know where we are and how to get to us. They see us at church or at the family dinner each week or maybe annually at the reunion. Whatever the frequency, their comments can be painful. Here are the classic family stingers. "Why aren't you married yet? What's wrong with you? Will I ever see any grandchildren?" Or the ever popular, "Can't you hold on to anybody?"

Family pressure is not a reason to want to get married. Your family members have an assortment of agendas why they are pressuring you to get married. You don't have the luxury of knowing what those are—just know that family members bring their own baggage to the topic of marriage. They may be dealing with a host of generational curses, such as divorce or separation, being hard to deal with, being too picky, or not being picky enough. Or they may just enjoy giving you a hard time. Don't marry just to please them. Instead, learn to deflect their darts (intentional or unintentional) and motivate yourself.

Whatever you do, don't let family pressure you into believing that marriage should be your utmost goal, as in the following case.

When I first began working with singles, I met a woman who was fixated on being married. Her obsession came from her parents, who instilled in her that she must have a husband by the time she finished high school. She grew up with the understanding that her worth was centered on marrying as soon as possible. When marriage did not occur after high school, her parents assured her of their love and said she could go to college and earn a "MRS." degree with the assurance that marriage would be eminent. They consoled her by saying, "We'll help you get closer to the wedding by purchasing the silverware as a wedding gift."

She went to college with the express purpose of meeting her future husband. Learning was secondary. She dated but never met just the right one until her final year. As her senior year ended, her boyfriend also ended their relationship. She was forced to graduate with only the college degree and not as a wife. Her parents patted her on the back and said, "It's okay. We know that you will marry soon. Why not go on to graduate school? Surely, there are some good catches there. In the meantime, we will help you out by purchasing all of your crystal stemware as a wedding gift."

She went to graduate school but emerged only with an advanced degree that did not help her advance down the aisle. Her parents consoled her again by saying, "Well, go out and get a job; surely you will meet someone to marry. We will help you out; we will purchase your china as a wedding gift." Yet no marriage proposal came her way. She was thirty-five years old and had everything for the wedding. Silver, crystal, china; she had everything but the man.

Ultimately all the pressure to marry became too much and she had a nervous breakdown. Her parents admitted her to a Christian psychiatric facility, where her counselor was able to diagnose her problem. She was operating in a mode that ran counter to what the Bible instructs us to do. She placed her desire for a husband first. God was not even on her list. She was instructed to "strive first for the kingdom and all [God's] righteousness, and all these things will be given to you as well" (Matt. 6:33). With the help of a Christian therapist, her life was re-ordered. God comes first. Next comes what God sends into her life. Today she is a happy woman with her priorities straight.

JEALOUSY OF MARRIED WOMEN

Envy cannot be your entrée to marriage. Envy is beneath you. God has given us so much; envy has no place in our queendom. If you are consumed with jealousy, you may wind up getting married because you want to show the world that you are eligible too and not because the right one has come along. When Carla was asked to be a bridesmaid for the twelfth time, she could not take it anymore. She had enough of being the proverbial bridesmaid and never the bride. The envy rose up in her like one of those squirting water fountains. She found it difficult to pretend to be happy for her engaged girlfriends. Jealousy pushed Carla into malice and she would make off-color remarks at the shower to embarrass the bride and noises during the wedding to distract the bride.

Sadly, Carla's envy was her undoing. She got married one day and it was done with the wrong motivation. "Finally he came along and, girl, I jumped on the opportunity to get married," she explained. "I was tired of waiting for my turn. He was talking right, saying all the things I wanted to hear. He had a job and looked half-decent. Why not? I thought. Well I wish someone had told me to slow down and quit trying to impress people," she said. "He was a dud."

Here is helpful advice from one woman, who was always a bridesmaid, to turn those occasions of being a bridesmaid into proactive, positive events that are free from jealousy. You too can turn the lemon into lemonade.

"I am a bridesmaid in my friends' weddings in order to meet more people," she wrote. I volunteer to be in charge of the guest book and offer to drive out-of-towners around. In my speech at the reception, I talk about how happy I am that the bride and groom have found each other and directly say to them, 'I hope one day I'll meet someone as wonderful as Mike.' What an opportunity to prompt the matchmakers in the room."[2]

FEAR OF BEING ALONE

There is a popular saying that says, "Misery loves company." If your primary reason to marry is because you can't stand yourself, then you've got a poor reason. I have discovered that a single woman who does not love herself will probably not love herself even if she is married. A single woman who does not enjoy her own company will continually look to her spouse to supply her joy, enthusiasm, and life.

Surely, a mate may contribute to this, but he is not ultimately responsible for it. You are. A woman with this disposition will be a most pathetic wife because she is so dependent on her mate for everything. She will also be prone to settling for anything or any type of man that comes along. I call these types of women, "the settling sisters." Yes, she has a man, but is he worth the trouble? Rather, she should exude a confidence that attracts. Whatever aura she puts out is the type that will come back. It's been said that the subconscious mind is programmed to recognize and attract what is familiar, not necessarily what is desirable. So, if you can't stand being with you, you will attract the same type of man. What a disaster that will be.

"The thought of spending one more day alone in the big 'ole house was too much for me," said Cheri. Her five-bedroom, five-bathroom, three-story home was inherited from an aunt. While the house was a dream house, living there was a nightmare for Cheri. "It did not feel right, so I found someone as fast as I could. But I guess I moved too fast. I had no idea that Ray was a drug addict. He seemed so nice and sweet. He was everything I was looking for, at least for a while. Then things went bad quick."

It was difficult for Cheri to end the relationship and put Ray out because it meant that she would be alone again. So she tolerated the situation. In her mind, it was better to have someone than no one at all.

YOUR BIOLOGICAL CLOCK IS TICKING

A woman's biological clock is defined as the tick-tock of the life clock inside her that indicates the time-sensitive ability to produce life. The built-in impulse may drive women into a state of anxiety and fear. Physically, something else urgent is going on. "Doctors generally believe that women are born with all the eggs they are ever going to have. As women age, eggs die off. The ones that remain are more likely to have chromosomal abnormalities that make an embryo (an egg fertilized by sperm), more likely to miscarry."[3] When we become aware of the ticking, we notice women with babies, and we wonder when, or if, we will ever be mothers.

Prolonged singleness aggravates the ticking. What complicates this is that, "According to the most recent U.S. census, more women than ever are electing to remain single (24 percent) and those who do have children later than ever (at the median age of 25.1, versus 21.4 in 1970). Because more women are postponing marriage and children as they focus their careers, many are finding themselves without a partner just as their reproductive capacity is waning.[4]

If single women decide to hearken to the ticking, some opt to use medical technology, and to their surprise they may face barriers. "The Atlanta-based Centers for Disease Control and Prevention reports that 16 percent of reproductive health-care providers in the United States routinely refuse to offer treatment to single women."[5] In order for single women to find doctors willing to help them, the cost of assisted reproduction can be prohibitively expensive. Artificial insemination, in which a woman uses donor sperm to get pregnant, can cost $500 to $5,000. In vitro fertilization, in which a woman's eggs are harvested from her body, fertilized with sperm, then implanted in her uterus, costs $25,000 to $75,000. One of the more cutting-edge options is cryopreservation, which is freezing the removed eggs while they are still viable. The average cost is $9,000.[6]

With 70 percent of births outside of wedlock in the African American community, single women are not so much bothered by the biological clock; they are beating it to the punch. Becoming a single mom by choice is the latest rage among African American, church-going women. They are simply tired of waiting on a good man to come along to start a family; so they start one without him.

"It looked like I was going to wait for a long time to marry and I did not want to miss the opportunity to have a child," said Kay, the twenty-four-year-old daughter of the pastor. "Yes, I would have preferred to be married and raise my son with a father, but this way at least I have a part of what I always wanted," says Kay. "In a way, I feel complete and whole. I am not as anxious about the future. In fact, I am very calm. Marriage is a nice option, but I know that it is not promised to me."

According to a *Washington Post* article, the number of single African American women who adopt is soaring. This highly personal decision reflects a national trend. Record numbers of single, professional black women have made similar choices in recent years, officials say, with profound implications for the nation's adoption systems.

"Forty percent of the [parents] who are adopting with our agency are single, black women," said Gloria King, executive director of the Black Adoption Placement and Research Center in Oakland, California, a city with a large African American population.

"They feel their biological clocks are ticking and they haven't married, but they want to parent," she said. "They're not going to let marriage stand in the way of them connecting with a child."[7]

Of the fifty thousand children of all ages permanently placed in U.S. homes through public adoptions in 2001, 32 percent were adopted by single women—and 55 percent of those women were black, according to the U.S. Department of Health and Human Services' Children's Bureau. The federal government figures show that half of the single, black women who adopted were between the age of thirty and fifty.[8]

Don't be pushed into marriage by the biological clock if you are not ready. Let's re-think the need to give birth outside of wedlock. This is not God's will for our lives. We have options. If you want a child, adoption is the best route to go.

BEING OUT OF CONTROL SEXUALLY

Let's be honest, sometimes it is just sex that you want and not a marital relationship. There is a difference. The biblical mandate "But if they are not practicing self-control, they should marry. For it is better to marry than to be aflame in passion" (1 Cor. 7:9) has driven many into marriage who should have remained single and taken a cold shower. We make a mistake if we lunge into marriage due to intense lust.

Sex should never motivate you to marry. The answer for you is getting your sex drive under control.

Sex is important, but not that important. Actually sex can block you from finding true love. "Sometimes sex is a consolation prize for people who despair of ever finding true intimacy. If they can't have the real thing then at least they won't settle for nothing at all. Rather than being an expression of desire, love, or connection, sex for them is an expression of fear and hopelessness."[9]

In counseling sessions with single women who are disconsolate over the bitter endings of their relationships, those who have the greatest difficulty moving on are those who were sexually active. Sex outside marriage can create an attachment that is uncontrollable despite conflicting expectations. The women say, "He is mine and I am his because we had sex. If we have sex, he will find me irresistible and marry me. Sex will create a bond between us." The men say, "Hey, I was horny that night and you were available. Sex never means love. It is a physical thing only."

Sex is putting the cart before the horse and can lead to broken hearts and weary spirits. Some women opt for the sex-only relationship. I wonder if they can handle this relationship long term?

"I told her from the start that I did not want a relationship. I only wanted sex and she said okay." Bruce explained. "I said it a second and third time and each time she said, 'I understand,' and was cool with it."

But after a few weeks, she said to me, "Well let's take this to the next level." Take what to the next level? There is nothing going on here to take anywhere. We agreed that this was sex only. What happened? "I didn't think you were serious."

This is a very serious matter. Serious harm can occur to a women's self-esteem when she willingly becomes a mere booty call. Her self-worth is shattered. To maneuver in this world, she will divorce her feelings from her reality—becoming cold and calloused. She must put her relationship with God on pause. The real problem is, when she finally encounters Mr. Right, she will not realize it or have the capacity to love him.

At a women's Bible study, Chloe stood and gave a powerful testimony. "I was messing around with a young man and having what I thought was the best sex in the world. But that was all we did. There was no relationship. We didn't realize that back then. We were young and dumb. He asked me to marry him and I said yes. The marriage did not last long because it was physical and nothing more."

Out-of-control sexuality is never a reason to marry. Sex outside of marriage will lead you into relationships, just not healthy ones.

Here are the top five reasons you may want to get married: having a happy self; having a healthy understanding of men; being healed from relationship wounds; having a single life that is together; and loving yourself. These reasons are built on a controlled want. Queens manage their wants; their wants do not manage them.

HAVE A HAPPY SELF

There is a gospel song that says, "I came to Jesus as I was, weary, worn and sad, and I found in him a resting place. He has made me glad." This song illustrates the power of Jesus to give us joy despite our circumstances. This is the best place to build your want for marriage. Right here, smack dab in the middle of Jesus joy, is the ideal genesis of your want for marriage. Having Jesus joy means you already have what you want and you are not overly worried about the rest. Nothing is more distressing than a dour, sour, single sister. She is mad at the world, angry about being single, and simmering to the point that if she gets one wrong look her way, there will be trouble. Happiness from God is the antidote for despair.

A happy self invites a happy man. A happy self is a celebration of who you are, and who can resist a great party? Decent men will want to join. And the busters will pass you by, knowing that you don't have time for their mess. Queen, you have the power to create your own happiness as a result of your connection to Christ. Manifest it every day by doing something meaningful for yourself. Don't wait on someone to do it for you. Let it be small, like putting on your favorite fragrance in the morning before leaving the house or eating a gourmet fruit plate at breakfast. Or purchasing the car you have had your eyes on for a while. You can construct that which brings you happiness. There is control here and that is an underlying cause of happiness.

Being happy or joyful must be a full-time goal. It sets the pace for others and keeps your "want" stable. It is a way of life. "You can't have a joy-filled life unless you have joy-filled minutes, hours, and days. . . . When you are 'in-joying' life you are in that moment, being instead of doing. And you are in a state of bliss instead of dissatisfaction or depression. Most of us are doing life—we're doing what pays the bills. Doing what we have to do, are expected to do, or are told to do. And not experiencing enough joy."[10]

HAVE A HEALTHY UNDERSTANDING OF MEN

Obtaining a healthy understanding of men for most of us will mean scraping off a lot of gook and going back to the beginning. I mean all the way back to the Bible, when God created Adam and Eve. God created man, then created woman, so I believe that we are cocreations. It is necessary to base our want here in this peaceful interpretation of men. Men are not better than us or less than us. We are both made in the image of God. "Let us make humankind in our image, according to our likeness . . ." (Gen. 1:26). Otherwise, the man frenzy will blow things way out of proportion and your wants will be needlessly exaggerated too. There are two common mistakes women make in their understanding of men. First, they erroneously elevate them to the level of gods, or second, they denigrate men to the level of sugar daddies.

As I travel, I hear women talk about men as though they were deities. It's almost like they were putting brothers on pedestals. They look up to them admiringly, in an almost worshipful way. When we cry out "Hosanna" to men, we place our salvation in their hands. Yet, the reality is that they cannot save us or offer us everlasting life. Rather, it is a sin to want a man so bad that we worship him. It is a distortion of how God designed us to relate to one another. It probably starts innocently. Comments like "He is so-o-o good looking; he is so-o-o wonderful" morph into praise and adoration that raises him up to an altar. In this place, a want can never remain stable. It will quickly get out of control.

Second, it is a good thing to learn that men were not put on earth just to buy us things and take us places. They are not our personal automatic teller machines that dole out cash at the push of a button. It cheapens their humanity and ours when we view them only for what they can do for us. This mindset is prompted by our materialistic society. We are encouraged to get all we can from a man. Some ask, "Why spend my money when I can spend his?" Queens don't go around looking for pockets to empty.

"You'd be surprised to know how many women are still stuck in that pattern of chasing men for superficial qualities. It may no longer be if he can dunk a basketball, but the prestige of the company he works for, or the amount of money he received in his bonus check last year."[11]

Understanding men in a healthy way and managing your wants will lead to the ever-useful ability to determine the good guys from the not-so-good guys. It's been previously said, and you would have to agree, that some good girls like bad boys. This means that inevitably women are drawn to a man who is referred to as a thug; a bad boy. Why does this happen? It's been said that there is a thrill when a woman dates a man with an edge. There is something called the thug appeal. It stems from the belief that he is strong and that he can protect us. The allure to the thug is similar to the magnetism we have towards other things we know we should not have, like outrageously caloric desserts or expensive designer shoes. Also some women love the challenge of a dangerous man. They believe that they can change him. We believe that no other woman has what we have. And what we have to offer, for example, our smile or our homemade peach cobbler, will tame him. More often than not, it is the woman who is changed. In some of the more depressive situations, we choose a roughneck in order to sabotage our lives. Deep down inside we know we will be mistreated, hurt, and abused. And we feel that we deserve this.

In her book *Do Not Talk to, Touch, Marry, or Otherwise Fiddle with Frogs,* Nailah Shami offers exceedingly clear insight into what separates a good man who is having a bad day from a bad man—or to use her terminology, a frog.

> *Good Man, Bad Moment:* Does an occasional sly double take when he sees an attractive woman.
>
> *Frog:* Passes out his pager number to attractive women.
>
> *Good Man, Bad Moment:* Is somewhat grumpy on Monday mornings.
>
> *Frog:* Calls you a "b" for using his hairbrush one morning.
>
> *Good Man, Bad Moment:* Fibbed about the number of girlfriends he had before you.
>
> *Frog:* Never told you he was still married to a woman in another state after five months of dating you.
>
> *Good Man, Bad Moment:* Gets a little testy the fifth time you ask him for his opinion of the new dress he's already convinced he praised you with, "You look great, babe."
>
> *Frog:* Slaps you because you bought a new dress.[12]

HAVE HEALED FROM YOUR RELATIONSHIP WOUNDS

Truth be told, a lot of us are walking around with open wounds from a painful relationship—not visible wounds, but inner, emotional, spiritual hurts from being mistreated, betrayed, abused, and more. It is not possible to manage your want with an open wound. The pain and agony will not permit you to give attention to or focus on anything else. Pain and agony are jealous; they do not like to share. You will need to heal first, and then manage your wants. Healing is moving beyond blaming others and self, and moving toward restoration. Forgiveness heals wounds and chases away pain. Forgiveness sweetens our lives because it adds flexibility to our spirits. It is a type of resiliency. Forgive, and you can refuse to be shaped by past negativity. Forgiveness also says that you have learned to handle life's disappointments and letdowns. No, you are not giving the person who hurt you the easy way out. Forgiveness does not erase the wrong done, it simply says, "I don't need to carry around that hurt anymore. It's just not worth it." The longer the hurt is carried the more intense the poison can become.

Shewanda Riley, author of *Love Hangover,* offers twenty signs that you may be over your love hangover:

1. You no longer are angry when you think about your ex.
2. You no longer are angry or feel hurt when you think about the relationship.
3. You no longer call [him] and don't accept [his] phone calls. You no longer have dreams, visions, fantasies about retaliation and revenge.
4. You no longer are distracted in your mind or asking about how your ex is doing.
5. You are able to talk about your ex without crying or getting emotionally upset.
6. You no longer yearn for the relationship to be reconciled and for things to be the way they were.
7. You can now look at pictures, cards, and souvenirs about the relationship without feeling angry, guilty, or shamed, etc.
8. You can enjoy your normal routine like work and/or school.
9. You no longer call your ex's home/jobs/friends and hang up.
10. You no longer drive by your ex's job/home hoping to catch a glimpse of him.
11. You no longer demand or expect an apology from your ex.
12. You embrace safe and healthy relationships with the opposite sex.

13. You no longer avoid public places . . . with the fear that you'll see "him."
14. Memories of the relationship bring a smile . . . not a sting.
15. You no longer fear and avoid intimacy.
16. You can accept both the good and bad things about the relationship and your ex.
17. You have regained your appetite and lost and/or gained weight.
18. Your sleeping patterns have returned to normal.
19. You no longer blame your ex for your current, past, or future relationship problems.
20. You drop all strategies to actively break up his/her new relationship.[13]

HAVE YOUR SINGLENESS TOGETHER

Having a single life that is together means you have a well-balanced life. You are not off kilter or overextended or frazzled. Rather, you are cool, unruffled, laid back, and composed. You've made peace with your single situation and see yourself as a whole, not a fraction waiting for the missing piece. This is another great place to manage your want. Your singleness is in concert—finally all the sections are in harmony. This is a place you can live for a while.

The balanced life reaps mightily. In her book *Trophy Man: The Surprising Secrets of Black Women Who Marry Well,* Joy McElroy writes that women who did marry were not women with, shall we say, raggedy lives. She used terms such as *grounded, firm grip on reality, spoke in terms of here and now, know how to live in the moment.* Such women, she said, "forced themselves to get a life. They were able to entertain, support, and motivate themselves. They ignored the fear of attending social events alone, realizing that if they didn't go by themselves, they might never go. They believed that their lives were what they made of them, and maximized their interests, hobbies, and social outlets when they did have boyfriends."[14]

Ask yourself this question, "Do you have a life?" A lot of us don't have a life because our finances have sucked the life out of us. In what shape are your finances? The condition of our money can often dictate the caliber of our lives. You have power here. It's up to you to use it. You should be in control of your money and not the other way around. Unfortunately some of us were not raised to be in control of money. Our money history follows us from childhood. If our parents had a relaxed, positive attitude about money, we may also. If they were closed and overly cautious about money; we may be also. Just talking about money is difficult.

Sometimes we are unable to take charge of our finances because we have money wounds. Those wounds can include "lack of self-love, not feeling worthy of having money, living a life out of harmony, and shopping to fill a void."[15] Financial advice duo Cheryl D. Broussard and Michael A. Burns say, "Whatever money wounds are crippling you and whether you are in or out of a relationship, raise your spirits by ceasing all attacks on your self-esteem. Tell your inner critics 'adios,' and begin to focus on positive solutions to alleviate your financial challenges. We aren't going to claim it will happen overnight. It can be a slow and difficult process."[16]

In addition to spending and saving well, most of all we must give back to God through our tithes. As believers in God, we are asked to give back to God 10 percent. "Bring the full tithe into the storehouse, . . . see if I will not open the windows of heaven for you and pour down for you an overflowing blessing" (Mal. 3:10). Some may believe that tithing starts once they get a husband. But it starts long before then. You and God need a special relationship based on your sacrifice. Your giving what is sacrificial demonstrates to God that you are serious about your faith and that you trust God to make a way in your life. A tithing single sister just makes sense.

One radio listener said to me, "I used to think that I would tithe after God blessed me and I waited and waited, but once I began, everything changed in my life. I found a sense of peace and joy inside of me."

Education is also a key to having a single life that is together. Our minds should be fed and not starved. The United Negro College Fund's motto applies to grown folk too: "A mind is a terrible thing to waste." Are you wasting your mind? You know that you are wasting your mind if you have a keen interest in a topic and do not pursue it. Have you left your high school degree unattained? Have you left your bachelor's degree incomplete? Do you have aspirations for a masters or doctoral degree? Attaining a degree gives your life a sense of satisfaction, not to mention it lifts your earning potential.

After her divorce, Mary went back to school on a mission. "I decided not to let the end of my marriage be the end of me. There is a community college near my home, so I enrolled. Yes, I was tired after work, but it made me feel proud to spend time on the campus with the students. They gave me energy and made me feel good about me."

LOVE YOURSELF

The Bible says, "Love your neighbors as yourselves." Instead we have a bachelor of arts degree in self-criticism, a master's degree in self-rejection, and we are working on completing a doctorate in self-destruction.[17] Self-love is the fifth method to best manage your want. A self that is madly in love with itself cannot be rocked or shocked by the desire for a man. Let's be clear about what self-love is and what it is not. It is not a narcissistic view of one's self. Narcissists believe that everything revolves around them and they are superior to all. Narcissism is anti-God because narcissists believe that they are better than God. Self-love is not this self-consumed, self-inflating addiction. I suggest that self-love is an affirmation and an acceptance of who you are. It is praising God for what God has done in you, with the faith that any flaws can be worked out by God in the future. The One who began a good work in you will endeavor to complete it.

Here are some things to show you and the world that you love you.

- Wake up in the morning and say, "Good morning, God!" Start off the day positive; refrain from saying "Good God, it's morning." Speak words of power and peace over your day before it begins.
- Get out of bed and go directly to a mirror. Look at your reflection, hug the person you see there, blow kisses to her, and say, "Hey, good looking!"
- Speak positive thoughts about your activities in the day ahead. "I will have a good day today." You can release positive feelings on yourself and your situation with uplifting words. Set the stage for the day to come with something good.
- Encourage yourself all day long. Keep a mental dialogue going that pats you on the back for things like getting to the office on time or making an effective presentation.
- Exercise is the ultimate manifestation of self-love. So many of us need the benefits that come along with daily exercise: relaxation, decreased stress, freedom from depression, increased circulation, and peace of mind.

Studies tell us that at least one-half of African Amercian women are overweight. This means that most of us are standing in the need of exercise and eating with more discipline. The link between exercise, eating right, and self-love is key for me. I have given all priority in my life. Regrettably, African American women are not as plentiful as we should be in the health clubs, on the tracks of local schools, or walking along city blocks. Often it is a hair issue. I do understand. We do not want to sweat out "the do" that took several hours waiting just to get done, and lots of dollars to pay for. Initially, I wore my hair in a style that was not exercise friendly. It prohibited me from strenuous exercise. I did not want to sweat it out and, as a result, I expanded dress sizes—but my hair looked good. Finally, after I could not fit into any of my clothes, I reprioritized my life. I changed my hair into a style that could be sweated. What a trade. It was easier to sit on the sofa and eat donuts than to go lift weights at the gym. Put down the donuts and spent four to five days per week in the gym. Even more, I invested in a personal trainer. She is someone who guides and monitors my exercise regime. You should see the looks that I get from some sisters when they learn that I have a personal trainer. They just don't get it. It's a love affair between me, myself, and I. The money I saved from the donuts goes a long way.

Queens, our health does not say, "I love you." According to Healthy People 2010, African Americans account for only 12 percent of the population in the United States, yet African Americans, as a group, have the poorest health status indicators in the nation and are disproportionately represented among underserved populations. Fifty-five percent of the 33.9 million African Americans in this country are women. Although there have been improvements in mortality rates, heart disease, stroke, and obesity, the health status of African American women continues to lag behind that of their white counterparts. African Americans continue to be two times more likely than whites to have hypertension, obesity, and high fat intake. Poor nutrition, smoking, and alcohol and drug abuse are reported to occur commonly in African American women, thereby increasing the risk for heart disease and type 2 diabetes. The lack of access to preventative care, a stressful lifestyle, poor education, inadequate housing, low-paying jobs, and a lack of insurance are powerful predictors of health outcomes.[18]

The journey to self-love can be made by all. Here is a poignant story from Jeanette. "First of all, I think the key to my healing from my divorce has been learning to love myself. Second is being able to accept that someone else could love me in the same way that I loved myself. Over the years, I have found that there are three things that we look for in a relationship with a man: affection, affirmation, and attention. Once you learn how to give those three things to yourself then you can allow someone else to come in your life and give those things to you as well. In fact, when you do that it will take the relationship to an entirely different level of fulfillment. During the process of receiving those things from someone else, trust begins to set in and it allows the relationship to continue to develop.

"After dealing with two failed marriages, I have come a long way. Yet I still have to admit that accepting *real* love from someone else is hard for me. Even learning to really love myself is an ongoing process. Yet it is continuous commitment to grow in that area, so that you can accept love from that special person. It doesn't happen overnight, but it does happen. I can't quite say that I am 100 percent there at this point. I guess that's why I am not married.

"Until I can openly and totally accept love and care from someone else, I will not be ready to take that final step in a relationship. Even today, there are always questions running in the back of my mind when I begin to let someone get close to me. I want to know: why is he treating me like this? What does he want? How long is this going to last? Last but not least, when is the other shoe going to drop?

"After all these years, trust is one of the issues that I still struggle with; however, one of the key components to me breaking through some of my barriers has been learning to love myself. In spite of my flaws and mistakes, I have had to genuinely learn to love me. All my life it has been about someone else: my parents, the children, and my husband. For me to cut through all of the negative thoughts the enemy had placed in me, I had to first love myself unconditionally. I had to realize that before I could affirm anyone else, I had to first affirm myself."

"When I first started getting pedicures, I thought it was the most selfish thing anyone could ever do. First I started giving myself pedicures and then treating myself to dinner. I started buying special things for myself to affirm myself. It was a slow process but a necessary process. I think women that do not learn how to appreciate themselves will accept any type of treatment from men.

"Now I know that it is important to have someone who is a part of my life affirm me as well. I think if I had not started to treat myself well I would not have been able to accept it from someone else. I know that I need someone in my life who will encourage me to do those things for myself. Small things like that add to the relationship and strengthen your bond. But, first and foremost, it all begins with loving yourself, and that is a day-by-day journey."

I pray that this chapter helped you revise your reasons for wanting to get married. Marriage is an honorable instiution, but should be approached wisely. Reject the reasons that stem from obession, and embrace the reasons that encourage you to utlize your wants.

QUESTIONS FOR REFLECTION

1. Have your reasons for wanting marriage changed after reading this chapter?
2. Do your family or friends pressure you to marry?
3. How big a role does sex have in your marital concerns?
4. Will unhealed wounds hurt your marital concerns?
5. Do you have a love hangover?
6. How do you show yourself that you love yourself?
7. How will you know if your singleness is together?

PRAYER

Revising God, I submit my thoughts to you and ask that you empower me to take a fresh look at my reasons for seeking to be married. Please protect me from obsessions and give me wants that I control. I don't want jealousy, fear of being alone, or a biological clock to drive me down the aisle. You and your peace are what I need. Amen.

5 · WHAT'S REALLY BOTHERING YOU?

It's easy to blame the gender imbalance or life in a boring city as reasons why you still are not married, but your emotional issues may actually be the culprit. Yes, sister, you have issues; all of us do. These are issues that hinder your readiness for a relationship. Your emotional trials may not seem troublesome because your momma and grandma wrestled with the same challenges. And it's familiar to you. They may be hereditary, passed down from one generation to the next, and still be in serious need of curtailing. There are women who are living the same pain as their ancestors without knowing it or without knowing that they can do something about it. These issues are harmful, but you are not aware of them because they are so deeply imbedded into your psyche or everyday patterns of life. Queens do something about their issues, lest their issues do something about them.

With more than twenty years dedicated to helping single women maximize their lives, I have experienced the hard way that mental health issues can cripple a woman who is trying her best to be the queen that God wants her to be. She can attend worship services faithfully, tithe, participate in weekly Bible study, and still be troubled. She can even be on her way toward answering God's call into ordained ministry, and yet be a prisoner of mental problems. I wrestled with this until I realized that the most I could do was to steer them toward mental health professionals. Some women wanted to cling to the pastor for a cure. This was futile and in vain and made me feel like a failure. As much as I wanted to see improvement and advancement in their lives, these could only come with mental health intervention.

In this chapter, to help you find out what is bothering you, I have compiled a number of mental and emotional concerns that are common among African American women. If you see yourself here, don't be ashamed. Activate yourself and seek help. If you see a friend or loved one here, ask her to read this book so she can help herself. You will learn about depression, obsessive compulsive disorders, panic disorders, and the addictions of alcohol, drug, shopping, and gambling.

There was Camile. She was diagnosed with clinical depression, ashamed of the diagnosis, yet tortured by the disease. She sought to supplement appointments with a psychologist and prescribed medication with pastoral visits to me. It was a nine-month period of great travail for her and for me. Her mental anguish became mine. I did not want to let her down as her pastor, but she was taking me in a downward spiral with her. Her demons became my demons. There is a better way for us—if only we will go.

Historically, African Americans have shunned professional help in the area of mental health. African Americans collectively have regarded psychological concerns as something that can and should be prayed away or ignored. There is a huge stigma attached to mental health care. There is embarrassment and shame attached to mental illness, along with its diagnosis and treatment. No one wants to be thought of as "crazy" or needing to go to the "nut house." We think that the "crazy" label will detour us from the possibility of marriage, when in fact, seeking a cure is actually what we need.

"There's a fear of putting our business in the street . . . of somehow revealing too much," said Latonya Slack, executive director of the California Black Women's Health Project. "Black women can perceive going to a therapist as something we don't do," she added.[1]

If we do seek mental health treatment, it is only when the illness is advanced and we are at our breaking point. Usually our pastors are the first persons we bring the trouble to. We tend to bring our concern to persons close to us first. "But at some point, the seriousness of some personal problems is likely to overwhelm the informal resources."[2]

Take Carrie, for example. She was the picture of business success. She had a chain of hair salons and a healthy bank account. She was attractive and physically fit, but she was on an emotional roller coaster all the time. She was happy and bubbly sometimes, and other times she was dismal and feeling suicidal. "But what is a single sister to do but keep moving and hoping for a better day," she said. Carrie was actually in the throes of serious mental distress, but she did not see the need to stop and address the matter. "It would clear itself up," she surmised. "Especially if I can find a decent man. All this will go away."

Unfortunately, lots of people think that all a single woman needs is a man to cure her troubles. That is a woefully simplistic answer and an egregious one that assumes male companionship cures all. If nothing else, this book will broaden your horizon concerning the needs of a single woman and her responsibility to take care of herself. Carrie is a classic example of the numerous women who blame their mental distress on being without a man, when in reality it is something much more serious.

DEPRESSION

Are you depressed? There's an obscene myth out there that African American women don't get depressed. We are supposed to be strong black women who can handle any and everything that life sends our way. False! We do experience depression. In large numbers. According to one media outlet, 60 percent of African American women suffer from depression.[3] Yet despite the high numbers, few ever seek treatment. Some estimate only 7 percent receive any treatment, compared with 20 percent of the general population.[4]

Don't get me wrong. There is a lot for us to be depressed about. I believe that legitimizing our causes for depression will help lift the shame. We lead frazzled, splintered, hurting lives. "Nationally, 43 percent of black women report they were verbally or sexually abused while growing up. Approximately 20 percent reported they were physically abused as a child and another 22 percent said they were sexually abused. Also, the poverty rate for black women is 25 percent, more than twice the rate among white women.[5] This is why we are depressed—but we don't have to stay there.

Here is a list of depressive symptoms:

- A depressed mood or loss of interest or pleasure that goes on for two weeks or more
- Significant weight loss or weight gain
- Significantly increased or decreased motor activity
- Fatigue or loss of energy
- Feelings of worthlessness or excessive or inappropriate guilt
- Diminished ability to think or concentrate; indecisiveness
- Hopelessness
- Recurrent thoughts of death or suicide[6]

The best definition of depression that I know is called "frozen rage." "If you have a consistently serious problem with depression, you have not resolved some area in your life. As surely as the night follows the day, depression follows unresolved, repressed, or improperly expressed anger."[7]

It should be noted that there are a variety of types of depression. Some come as a result of giving birth; others result from a change in the weather or from the monthly menstrual cycle. *Postpartum depression* comes after the delivery of a baby for some women. *Seasonal affective disorder* means your depression comes in the fall and winter and ends in the spring.[8] Once a month, some sisters come unglued with *premenstrual syndrome,* or *premenstrual depression* (PMD). PMD is a depressive disorder that may cause irritability and a sad mood for a week or more before your period, which is resolved with menstrual flow.[9]

You may have PMD if you have five of the following symptoms during the premenstrual week and the symptoms resolve within the first few days of your menstrual flow:

- Sad, gloomy feelings, including feeling worthless or useless
- Abrupt mood swings, with sudden tears, anger, or personal oversensitivity
- Diminished ability to concentrate
- Low energy, getting tired too easily
- Sugar, salt, or junk food cravings
- Feeling overwhelmed or unable to manage things you usually can handle[10]

Your depression may have in fact been triggered by an illness. A prime example of this is diabetes, which affects some 2.2 million African Americans, the majority of whom are women. "Some studies have found that 40 percent of diabetics also have clinical depression. Either disease can strike first. Women who are depressed may give up exercising and overeat to the point of developing diabetes. Women who already have diabetes may develop depression. Depression adversely affects how the body responds to insulin."[11]

OBSESSIVE-COMPULSIVE DISORDER

"Obsessive-compulsive disorder (OCD) is characterized by persistent, disturbing, unwanted thoughts, obsessions (impulses or images), and compulsions (repetitive and ritualistic thoughts or actions which the individual feels compelled to perform).[12]

It is more likely found in women than men and may include repetitions such as "checking the door, hand washing, praying, counting or repeating words—all done with the goal of preventing and reducing anxiety or distress."[13]

A young college coed began to exhibit what was ultimately diagnosed as OCD when she came to the college clinic with complaints of hair loss. While sitting in the waiting room of the clinic she was observed ritually pulling the hairs from her head. She had a number of stressful situations in her life and they impacted her socially and academically. Not only was she pulling the hair from her head, she kept them and counted them nightly as a part of her ritual to relieve stress and anxiety. She progressed well with treatment.[14]

PANIC DISORDER

Panic disorder (PD) is defined as experiencing palpitations, sweating, trembling or shaking, shortness of breath, feeling of choking, chest pain, nausea, dizziness, tingling sensations, hot flushes, or chills.[15] It comes from victimization, and unfortunately, African American women are victims of rape and domestic violence at a higher rate than other ethnic groups.[16] Along with the victimization comes the pronounced fear of being called crazy, which causes persons who suffer with PD to be secretive about the disorder.[17]

In a study of African American women with PD it was noted that they decided not to seek treatment for two reasons. One was that they believed that "the anxiety was a part of their lives." They opted to pray it away and use faith and in some instances mind-altering substances to cope.[18] The other reason was that the women made "a conscious choice not to acknowledge" their anxiety-related feelings because doing so would be admitting that they had a problem. One woman stated, "Baby, I don't have time to think about that mess. If I did I'd worry about everything."[19]

As a pastor and counselor, I am encouraged to follow the suggestions of mental health professionals to broaden the scope and depth of women's programming in the church. We need more than prayer and

Bible study. After we pray and read we need mental health programming. They suggest that there should be "programs to enhance coping skills, to improve social management skills, and to encourage health promotion. Enhancement of coping skills may be especially important because black women tend to experience appreciably higher levels of stress than white women. . . . Strategies for making and maintaining friendships—specific communication skills such as active listening and nondefensive responding—could enhance the quality of social support."[20]

I believe that these recommendations can greatly improve the state of mental health among African American single women and relieve some of our needless stress.

WHAT YOU SHOULD DO NOW

If you are experiencing the signs of mental or emotional distress, you should take action. The longer you wait to determine if you need help, the more detrimental your situation may become. If could be the root of your problems with men. One caller asked this related question.

Dear Dr. Patterson,

I am a Christian. I have been married twice before and it seems like every man that I meet leaves me. I starting dating again, and I meet Christian men, but the ones that I meet don't stick around long. Why does every man that I meet leave me? Can you give me any insight as to why this keeps happening to me?

Left Behind

Dear Left Behind,

It sounds like your problems may be below the surface. The two marriages and the way the guys are not sticking around says that something is not adding up with you mentally. Please don't be offended, but I suggest that you visit a counselor for help and to get answers to your questions.

Visit with a medical doctor, share your concerns, and ask for a basic diagnosis. The doctor will be able to make a general observation and if there is cause can connect you with a psychologist to assist you further. If you do see a psychologist, she or he will offer you a battery of tests to determine the presence and depth of the illness. At that point it will be determined what course of action is needed. Counseling, medication, or both can be used to relieve your symptoms. Don't look for an overnight cure and a quick fix. We are dealing with your precious mental health and there is no need to rush. Take your time and allow the process to work. If you have supportive family and friends, allow them to accompany you on this journey. Be patient, and most of all be prayerful.

WOMEN AND ADDICTIONS

Addictions invade your mind and warp your emotions. If you are addicted it will rob you of the person that you once were. Being addicted to something could be what's bothering you. The following description of addictions speaks to many single women. "Addiction is based on the fulfillment of needs that you are not getting fulfilled in other ways."[21] You are susceptible to addiction if you lack the staples of existence, the sustenance that life offers people under normal conditions. You are primed for addiction when you lack the social supports of friends and family, inner security and peace of mind, and options for fun and constructive work. That is, you are most at risk for addiction when you do not have the following elements in your life:

- Family and friends
- satisfying work
- enjoyable pastimes
- a positive environment
- a belief in your personal value
- involvement in a community
- a purpose in life[22]

DRUG AND ALCOHOL ADDICTION

Drug and alcohol addiction is widespread due to the pain of life. Many women turn to a substance to help them make it through. "An estimated 22 million people in the U.S. struggle with alcohol and drug addiction, and 9.5 percent of them are African American."[23] We can lose our jobs, our children, and our lives due to an addiction. Someone who saw this firsthand is Lucy Hall. She lost her mother to alcoholism at the age of six, and herself struggled with drug abuse. According to an article in *Essence*, Hall gave birth to her first daughter in 1989 and left the infant in the hospital to go and get high. This savvy woman went on to turn her pain into passion and purpose. She founded a residential treatment facility in Atlanta for women who are addicted to drugs or alcohol. She won the nation's highest honor for community health leadership, and she herself was an addict.

Hall was working as a housekeeper and volunteering as a counselor in Atlanta when she launched a plan to help women struggling with substance abuse. Using seed money from her employer, she founded a residential recovery program called Mary Hall Freedom House in memory of her mother. Hall soon realized that addicted women with small children had little access to residential treatment because most programs did not admit children. She revamped Freedom House to create Atlanta's only residential recovery program for women with children. Women in the program undergo intensive chemical dependency treatment, while their children take part in prevention programs to help them avoid falling into a family substance-abuse pattern.

Signs of Drug and Alcohol Abuse

Physical Signs

- Change in sleeping patterns
- Bloodshot eyes
- Slurred or agitated speech
- Sudden or dramatic weight loss or gain

- Skin abrasions/bruises
- Neglected appearance/poor hygiene
- Sick more frequently
- Accidents or injuries

Behavioral Signs

- Hiding use; lying and covering up
- Sense that the person will "do anything" to use again regardless of consequences
- Loss of control or choice of use (drug-seeking behavior)
- Loss of interest in previously enjoyed activities
- Emotional instability
- Hyperactivity or hyperaggression
- Depression
- Missing school or work
- Failure to fulfill responsibilities at school or work
- Complaints from teachers or co-workers
- Reports of intoxication at school or work
- Furtive or secretive behavior
- Avoiding eye contact
- Locked doors
- Going out every night
- Change in friends or peer group
- Change in clothing or appearance
- Unusual smells on clothing or breath
- Heavy use of over-the-counter preparations to reduce eye reddening, nasal irritation, or bad breath
- Hidden stashes of alcohol
- Alcohol missing from your supply

- Prescription medicine missing
- Money missing
- Valuables missing
- Disappearances for long periods of time
- Running away
- Secretive phone calls
- Unusual containers or wrappers[24]

What You Should Do

In seeking help, please consider a drug or alcohol rehabilitation center. These treatment facilities offer detoxification and assistance kicking the habit. You will need professional help changing your addictive behavior. One option to remain free of the addiction is Alcoholics Anonymous or Drugs Anonymous. Chapters of these organizations can be found in many places, such as churches or community centers. They are free.

SHOPPING ADDICTION

Girlfriend, a shopping addiction sounds like fun until you find yourself buying things you know you don't want or need because you can't help yourself. "Psychotherapists explain that millions of Americans shop excessively out of boredom, anxiety, anger, joy, or fear of being hurt—in other words every human feeling."[25]

When shopping is out of control, it becomes a secret obsession. Money gets borrowed, credit cards are maxed out, bills go unpaid, and lies get told. Shame and guilt become constant companions and fear of discovery haunts the addict at every turn. Often, purchases of useless items are hidden—put away and never used.

Shay can admit the truth now—five years after the fact. Her out-of-control spending crushed her marriage. "I could not help myself, and Roderick did not understand my needs. I am a grown woman and can do what I want to do. He had no right to try and control me," she said. Daily, the trunk of her car was crammed with items bought that day. "I bought on a secret credit card that I applied for by myself," she explained. "I'd hide the bills and shop away. The trouble started when the creditors called."

Shay reluctantly enrolled in a shopping addiction therapy group and was helped greatly. "I saw what my issues were and I saw a way out. I cut up all the credit cards. I am a cash only woman. I can even see getting back with Roderick, if he will have me," she said.

Psychologist Dr. April Benson founded a helpful organization called Stopping Overshopping to offer a way out for those with problematic buying behavior. Her website www.stoppingovershopping.com asks a series of questions to help determine whether a person might have compulsive shopping issues prefacing the list with the question "Are you one of America's 15 million shopaholics?"

- Do you use shopping as a quick fix for the blues?
- Do you spend more than you can afford?
- Are some of your purchases unused or hidden?
- Do you feel guilty or ashamed about this behavior?
- Would your life be richer if you were shopping less?
- Have your attempts to change been unsuccessful?[26]

What Should You Do?

Shopping addicts must seek professional counseling to deal with this problem. Don't try to cure yourself. The experts say that often the addictions may come in groups or clusters. You may be dealing with more than one.

GAMBLING ADDICTIONS

Do you play the lottery in your loneliness? Do you take a trip to the casino to make yourself feel better about being single? You could be a woman with a gambling problem. Women sometimes use gambling "as a way to avoid loneliness, painful emotions, and difficult life situations" making them "vulnerable to developing gambling problems.[27] Women are vulnerable to becoming problem gamblers when they are trying to:

- Minimize loneliness
- Escape emotionally from past or current traumas
- Escape physically from chronic pain, addiction, or other health problems
- Get out of poverty by winning money
- Avoid conflict or abuse at home
- Relieve stress[28]

One statistic is amazing. It states that "people who earn less than $10,000 a year buy more tickets than any other income group, and the proportion of family income spent on the lottery goes up as family income goes down."[29]

The way I see it, gambling, whether it is the lottery or casinos or even bingo, can be an addiction. It is addictive because some sisters are looking for the magic that will change their lives. The instant money and fame is improvement without any effort. We know, however, that quick fixes usually don't work.

What You Should Do

A woman with a gambling problem should seek counseling and referrals to debt counselors. One good source is Gamblers Anonymous. It worked for Loretta.

"Those church trips to the casinos started off as innocent fun," said the sixty-something grandmother. "But something got a hold of me after my husband died. I started going up there on my own. I'd take a handbag full of cash, lose it, and not care about the mortgage. Betting made me forget the pain. I just about lost the house. I was close to eviction when the pastor got word. The deacons came by and saved me. We prayed and everything. But they said the only way they'd help me out was if I went to Gamblers Anonymous. I did not want to go because I did not see the problem, but I wanted the help. I need it."

I know something is bothering you and I want to help you find out what it is. In this chapter I compiled a number of mental and emotional concerns that are common with African American women. You learned about depression, obsessive compulsive disorders, panic disorders, and the addictions of alcohol, drug, shopping, and gambling. Reading this chapter has probably been challenging. I pray that this material opened your eyes and touched you. I presented this material to meet an unspoken need in your life. This is not a topic discussed at the hair salon or the nail shop. It is too personal. Thank you for allowing me into your space.

QUESTIONS FOR REFLECTION

1. Is something bothering you? Do you know what it is?
2. Why do people think a man will solve psychological problems?
3. Who is the person to whom you would take a mental health concern?
4. What would motivate you to seek help?
5. What are you addicted to?
6. Why do some women get high/drunk to ease their loneliness?
7. How can a shopping addiction ruin a relationship?

PRAYER

Healing God, I now understand that if something is bothering me, it is bothering you too. I want to bravely face my issues. Strengthen me to look at them and seek professional help for them. You don't want me to live like this. Amen.

6 · YOU'D BETTER HAVE IT

Queens, your bags need to be packed with the essential tools that will assist you in the journey of being all that God wants you to be. In this chapter, I'll share vignettes of biblical truths to inspire you and empower you. You require an array of tools to keep the crown on your head and not drop it by doing something self-destructive. This is no small feat! You will need the following skills: a solid self-concept, the strength to confront your demons, the knowledge that God will deliver you, the ability to endure, the power to climb higher than your problems, a willingness to work for God, and a mature attitude. I have compiled a list of indispensable skills you will need. These skills can't be purchased in a store. They are developed over time and with a relationship with God.

YOU'D BETTER HAVE A SOLID SELF-CONCEPT

A solid self-concept means that you have to see yourself as God sees you. Queens keep this in the front of their arsenal and use it constantly. Our society praises the richest, prettiest, and most powerful.

If that does not describe us, we may tend to feel less than worthy. When we feel "less than," we act less than, and trouble usually follows.

Here is where our solid self-concept has to swing into action to undergird us with stability lest we fall. If left unchecked, the "less than" feelings can grow into what I call the grasshopper syndrome. In Numbers 13:33 we read these words, "And to ourselves we seemed like grasshoppers, and so we seemed to them." The grasshopper syndrome came upon the spies who were sent to check out the land that God had promised them. The spies took note of the lush fruit and the fertile soil and what appeared to be the large people (verses 27-28). They saw people and considered them stronger and better just because they were different. They became intimidated.

When we have the grasshopper syndrome, we doubt God's goodness in us and we question why we were made the way we are. The grasshopper syndrome means that we are green, small-minded, and always jumping to conclusions. Being green means that we can be filled with jealousy and envy. Jealousy and envy occur because we want what someone else has, and we forget that God is generous and will provide for us as well.

Being small-minded means that people and places can belittle us. They don't actually have to be proportionally larger than us, but they make us feel diminished. Small-mindedness means that we are unable to see God's big picture. A small-minded person refuses to see the greatness that God has for them.

Finally, like the jumping grasshopper, we may quickly jump to conclusions because we are insecure. We don't feel good about ourselves and don't feel comfortable asking questions.

To remedy the grasshopper syndrome, realize that you are better than any insect. You are better today than you were yesterday, and you will be better tomorrow than you were today. You can release the grasshopper syndrome by getting rid of the fear of others. You are giving them too much power over your life.

Can I tell you a story about me? I pastored a church that was located in the middle of a tract of land owned by wealthy developers.

The developers announced a hundred million dollar plan to build skyscrapers with high-rise apartments, retail stores, and restaurants—all around the church. When I heard about it, I felt overwhelmed and "less than" because neither I nor my church had millions of dollars. My solid self-concept resuscitated me. I had to learn that new situations don't have to be threatening. I recalled that when new situations come along, they don't have to knock us down. I am a firm believer that we are promoted by our persecutions, and strengthened by our struggles.

YOU BETTER HAVE THE STRENGTH TO CONFRONT YOUR DEMONS

Demons will distract you from your goals and purpose. Queens have the strength to confront demons because of Christ. We are not alone in our confrontation. It begins with confessing our mess. Many of us have demonstrated evil behavior or self-destructive thought. All of us have demons or negative inner issues. Come out of denial about your situation. If we want to fix it, we must first face it. We cannot conquer what we cannot confront. No matter how long we have been Christians or how many tongues we speak in, we all have to admit our unchristian behaviors (lying, cheating, gossiping, and the like). If we do not dismiss them, they will destroy us. If we are unwilling to identify and confront the major issues of our lives, we cannot be what God is calling us to be. We'll be second-rate copies. If we are willing to identify them, God will move them out of our lives.

Jesus encountered a man who had not been able to successfully deal with his demons—see Luke 8:26–39. As a result of the demonic possession, the young man preferred to live naked in a graveyard (verse 27). This means that our issues can drive us away from the people we love and also strip us of all dignity. Pause for a second and take note of how you are living. Ensure that you are not living among dead things—such as dead hopes, dead dreams, and dead people.

It is interesting to note that the demons knew who Jesus was without an introduction. The demon said, "What have you to do with me, Jesus, Son of the Most High God? I beg you, do not torment me" (verse 28). If the devil knows who Jesus is, we had better make sure that we know him even more. Do we know Jesus as our way maker? As our burden bearer and our heavy load sharer? Ensure that you keep the relationship alive by constant conversation with Jesus.

After a conversation with the demons, Jesus drove them out of the man and into a herd of pigs. The pigs promptly killed themselves by going headfirst into a lake. Once the man was set free, the first thing he did was sit at the feet of Jesus. This is the best place to be when Jesus heals you. It's a humble position and a safe position. A queen is also seated at the feet of Jesus. There she can receive godly instruction on her next moves in life.

The illustration of Jesus and the demons is good news to us because we certainly need spiritual relief. It shows us that Jesus is the only one who can fix our situation.

You should know that the fight between Jesus and the demons was a fixed fight. A fixed fight has the winner determined in advance. You don't have to worry too much about what will happen when God has it all under control. You can even take a nap because the outcome has been arranged. You can be calm, cool, and collected for the entire battle. The best part of this parable is the ending. Jesus instructed the healed man to go and tell everyone. He said, "Return to your home, and declare how much God has done for you. So he went away, proclaiming throughout the city how much Jesus had done for him" (verse 39).

This means to us that once God rids us of our demons, we can't sit back and get cute. We should go and tell the world about our healing. The people who saw us when we were lying need to see us speaking the truth. The people who saw us causing constant chaos need to see that we can be peacemakers. Go and tell them.

YOU'D BETTER KNOW THAT GOD WILL DELIVER YOU

Queen, the longer you live, the more obstacles you will face. Please consider them as practice fields for your victory. This knowledge will carry you when you can't carry yourself. It will motivate you when you can't put one foot in front of the other just to move an inch. Throughout the Bible, God's people were constantly facing what appeared to be insurmountable obstacles. Every time, however, God made a way out of no way. Insurmountable odds are a part of life. They build us up, not tear us down. The key is that despite the darkest night or fiercest storm, we have to believe that God will deliver.

Let's focus on the children of Israel who were enslaved by the Egyptians. The Egyptians were cruel slave masters who forced them to work in inhumane ways. God heard their cries and appointed Moses to lead them into freedom. This tells us that God hears our cries and sets our rescue in motion. Never think that your cries go unheeded.

God delivers more than the U.S. Postal Service! They take pride in their slogan that they bring the mail through rain, sleet, or snow. God can top that. The Israelites escaped Egypt by way of the wilderness. It looked like they were stuck between the Red Sea and Pharaoh's army, but they weren't. As they stood facing the Red Sea, God told Moses to tell the people, "Do not be afraid, stand firm, and see the deliverance that God will accomplish for you today; for the Egyptians whom you see today you shall never see again. God will fight for you, and you have only to keep still" (Exod. 14:13–14).

The scriptures say the sea was parted. God's hands came along and separated the powerful waters and gave the Israelites safe passage. There are bodies of water in front of you right now. It seems there is no way you can cross them. Don't worry. Our God will part them and you will walk across on dry land. You won't have to get your pumps muddy!

God was a deluxe deliverer to the children of Israel. When God brought them out of bondage, God shielded them from the desert's hot sun with shade by the day. At night, God kept the cold off them by being a pillar of fire. When God brings you out of a situation, you will be taken care of. You won't have to worry how it will be done or where it will be done. You can rest in the knowledge that it will be done.

Along the journey with God, the Israelites complained. Can you imagine? God liberated them from bondage, and they griped. Some said that they would rather have stayed in Egypt. Others questioned what God was doing and they said to Moses, "Was it because there were no graves in Egypt that you have taken us away to die in the wilderness?" (Exod. 14:11). This Exodus illustration should excite and delight us with the news that help is on the way.

YOU'D BETTER HAVE THE ABILITY TO ENDURE

Queens realize that they need to hang in there and outlast tough times. We need to be able to take the heat. There is a popular saying: "If you can't take the heat, get out of the kitchen." Kitchens are hot, steamy places because baking, cooking, and frying can be done at the same time. You can fry fish on the front eye of the stove, have a pot of collards on the back eye of the stove, and have a macaroni and cheese casserole in the oven. That's a hot kitchen! Sometimes life is equally hot with bills, kids, health concerns, and more. We have options. We can stay or we can leave. God says stay and endure because there are blessings on the other side.

The Old Testament prophet Jeremiah was living in a time that seemed like a hot, stifling kitchen. Idolatry was rampant. The people had turned away from God. Life was not going well. He called on God for comfort. He asked pointed questions about his situation. "Why does the way of the guilty prosper? Why do all who are treacherous thrive?" (Jer. 12:1). Much to his surprise, God did not offer a soft and cuddly response. God did not say, "I'm sorry about your troubles. Here is a tissue and a hug." Rather, God said, "If you have raced with foot-runners and they have wearied you, how will you compete with horses? And if in a safe land you fall down, how will you fare in the thicket of the Jordan?" (12:5).

I suggest that God is doing us a favor with this tough talk. This personal and practical line of questioning is the wake-up call. We need to prepare to endure in order to win the prize. If our faith is not equal to the ordinary emergencies of each day, then what will you do when you come to that extraordinary day? If you cry over a paper cut, how will you handle a real scrape or bruise?

In this text, I hear God telling us to toughen up because we have a race to run. God is saying, "Queens, you had better run. " As a queen, there is a time to style and profile in elegant clothes. And there is a time to don our athletic shoes and gym clothes and get moving. "Every day in Africa, a gazelle wakes up knowing that it must outrun the fastest lion or it will die. Every day in Africa, a lion wakes up knowing that it must run faster than the slowest gazelle or it will not eat. It doesn't matter whether you are a gazelle or a lion, every day you wake up, and you must run.[1]

Let me share my secret for enduring. One cold winter day, I was about to enjoy a cup of hot tea. As I held the tea bag just above the steamy water, it spoke to me. It said, "Sheron, you are a lot like me." I responded, "Tea bag, how am I like you?" The bag answered, "We both have a lot of flavor, but it only comes alive when we come in contact with hot water. The hotter the water, the better your ability to make a difference! With the hot water comes faith, trust, love, devotion, and more. Don't be afraid of the hot water!"

YOU'D BETTER LEARN TO CLIMB HIGHER THAN YOUR TROUBLE

Queen, you need deer feet. No, I am not suggesting any type of newfangled surgery. In the obscure Old Testament book of Habakkuk, the prophet says that he can rise above hard times because he has feet like a deer. He can climb higher than his trouble. He writes, "I will exult in the God of my salvation. God, the Lord is my strength; he makes my feet like the feet of deer, and makes me tread upon the heights" (Hab. 3:19).

When difficulties arise, remember that you don't have to be overtaken. God will give us feet like a deer so that we can walk on the rocky, steep, untreadable areas. You see, the deer is a unique animal—and so are we. It has long thin legs, which make it a good runner. The deer's foot is really two center toes. Each of the toes is protected by a hard covering called a hoof. A deer runs on tiptoe with a springing or bouncing motion. The deer is uniquely designed to roam in the high, rocky places that others cannot visit. It is protected and safe in those places. It must be fearless in its journey upward and not concerned about how it will make it or if it is prepared. God has already equipped the animal and so it moves automatically. When God has already equipped us, why don't we forge ahead? When God prepares our feet, we should breathe a sigh of relief. We know it will be okay. Sure footing means that we will arrive. God does not "let our feet slip" (Psa. 66:9); God keeps our feet from falling (Psa. 56:13).

I once heard about a Sunday school teacher who was retiring from years of distinguished teaching. It was the church's tradition to frame and hang a photo of the retiring teachers on a classroom wall. This was done and the retiring teacher was well pleased. She came to the class on the next Sunday and noted that someone had knocked her photo off the wall. Alarmed, she went to the pastor with her concern. The pastor responded, "You've got some enemies around here. Hang your photo higher next time." She returned to the class and did so. The next Sunday she came back to the class and noted that her photo had been knocked down again. Alarmed, once more she went to the pastor. The response was the same; she complied and hung it even higher on the wall. When the teacher came to the classroom on the following Sunday, she was relived to see that her photo was still hanging. Joyfully she informed the pastor, who said, "I guess you finally went so high that you were out of their reach." We can be a high climber with God. Don't be afraid of the height. That's where our safety is.

YOU'D BETTER BE A WILLING WORKER FOR GOD

As a queen you must care for others and be actively involved in making a difference in the world. Something has to happen inside us to cause the concern for others. It is not automatic. The feelings start inside with a relationship with Jesus. Even though it's vital, it also feels good to do God's work, but if we are not careful, we may end up as spectators in the church. We erroneously think that someone else will get the work done. Too many people sit, listen, and do nothing more. Our response to a stirring sermon or a time of fervent prayer should be action. We've got to do something. It's no time for bench warming.

In Isaiah 6:1–5, we have the compelling incident of a bench warmer converting into a willing worker. The passage concludes with Isaiah waving his hands, jumping up and down, and proclaiming, "Here am I; send me!" (verse 8). God put a participating spirit or awakened a participating spirit inside of Isaiah. Without it, God could do nothing with him. If God is not in you, you will not feel compelled to help anyone. You would rather sit at home or concentrate on your best interests.

Let's observe the process that God used. First Isaiah had a close encounter with God. That is, he met God for himself and gained faith. His was not a borrowed faith or a facsimile faith. It was real and it belonged to him. The encounter was a bit terrifying. Isaiah saw God in the temple "high and lofty" (verse 1).

Second, once Isaiah saw God he was transformed because he saw his true self. When we look at God, we also are humbled. The greatness of God brings us to our knees. Isaiah said, "Woe is me! I am lost; for I am a man of unclean lips; yet my eyes have seen the King, the Lord of Hosts!" (verse 5). In order to serve God properly, we must be humble. An arrogant, conceited, puffed-up person is difficult to work with. God is looking for those with humble, teachable spirits. Humble people make the best servants. If no one can tell you anything, how can God? If you know everything, why do you need God?

"It's been said that the true way to be humble is not to stoop until you are smaller than yourself, but to stand at your real height against some higher nature that will show you what the real smallness of your greatness is."[2]

Finally, Isaiah was brought to participation because he allowed God to remove those things that were unacceptable from his life. "The seraph touched my mouth with it and said: 'Now that this has touched your lips, your guilt has departed and your sin is blotted out.'" (verse 7). This tells us that one way or another God wants to remove those things that separate us, so that we can freely and willingly and joyfully serve.

YOU'D BETTER HAVE A MATURE ATTITUDE

Queens are grown women, not little girls. Period. Yet we live in a time when it's popular and acceptable not to grow up. Grown people are clinging to childish ways and juvenile behavior. Immaturity is celebrated as the "in" thing, but God calls us to set a higher standard and grow up. Despite God's call, some of us are not as mature as we should be due to arrested development. Many are caught up in inappropriate behavior; others follow false doctrine. That's why Paul wrote in Ephesians 4:14, "We must no longer be children, tossed to and fro and blown about by every wind of doctrine, by people's trickery, by their craftiness in deceitful scheming."

We are on God's timetable of growth. Some are children who are wise beyond their years. Some are adults who have minds like babies. Some have no degrees and are brilliant, while others have Ph.D. degrees and are merely educated fools. Due to the widespread arrested development in the church, we have the phenomena of babies raising babies. These are spiritually young Christians attempting to raise other young Christians. It's like the blind leading the blind, heading nowhere fast. A baby can only take you as far as she has been. A seasoned mature teacher is needed.

We grow up by realizing that there is a purpose behind every problem. Instead of saying, "Why me?" grow up and look for the lessons in life. I am not suggesting that our God enjoys inflicting pain. It is true that we learn more lessons in the house of pain than the house of joy. God could have kept Deborah out of battle, Hagar out of the wilderness, and the woman at the well from being divorced multiple times. But that was not God's plan. Each of those women went through something and came out better on the other side.

Growing up can be painful, that's why some avoid it. There is struggle. It is not comfortable. It aches as you grow. We've got to accept our growing pains. There are no shortcuts to maturity. It's got to be God's way.

QUESTIONS FOR REFLECTION

1. What childish ways are you clinging to?
2. What are the benefits of growing up?
3. Have you ever been intimidated by a person you did not even know or just met?
4. What are your spiritual behavior challenges? Are you a liar, cheater, gossiper? Something else?
5. How do you hold onto the belief that God is a deliverer?
6. How hot is your kitchen? Do you plan on staying or leaving?
7. Are there things that stand between you and serving God?

PRAYER

God of Growth, help me to pack my bag with all the essentials. I need an array of skills that come from you. Make me open, accessible, and humble to your direction. Amen.

7 · FOCUS FRANKLY ON FRIENDSHIPS

Quality friendships are essential to a queen. She requires friends who are worth their weight in gold. Otherwise, they can be real stinkers and hindrances to her search for self-esteem and self-definition. Friends supply the wants and needs in the single woman's life so she must ensure that she includes the best. Friends help a queen diffuse the need for a man in her life. If she has buddies, life can be much more bearable.

This chapter will teach you how to examine the depth and breadth of your current friends and how to improve and enhance them to mutual satisfaction. The goal is that you would value the friendships of other women and understand how they can help you. Together we will explore biblical views on friendships, loneliness, television images of African American women friends, the levels and types of friends, friends in motherhood, married friends, social friends, church friends, friends online, and how to be a friend.

A woman without friends may say that she is lonely. "When women talk about being lonely, they may in fact be talking about the loneliness that comes from not having a full and embracing friendship network. When women are content with their lives, they may wish they had a partner, but they don't necessarily dwell on his absence. Therefore, to feel grounded in your present life (as opposed to living for the future), you need a rich social life."[1]

The Bible provides numerous images of friendship. One of the more compelling examples is found in Mark 2:3–5. Here four friends carried their paralyzed friend to see Jesus. The size of the crowd surrounding Jesus prevented them from getting close to the house where he was speaking. The friends were determined to give their sick friend an opportunity to see Jesus and they stopped at nothing. Verse 4 says that they removed the roof and dug a hole and lowered their friend down to Jesus. When Jesus saw their devotion to the sick man, he declared him healed. The love and attention from friends can heal us too.

Additionally, the scriptures tell us that "a friend loves at all times" (Prov. 17:17). This means that you should be a consistent friend. Not one who only shows up in the good times. You should also demonstrate unconditional love.

The Bible warns that you don't need a great number of friends. "Some friends play at friendship but a true friend sticks closer than one's nearest kin" (Prov. 18:24). This is wisdom concerning the need to run with a crowd. As we mature, we should lose the desire to associate with and travel in large numbers of people. Be selective concerning whom you are seen with and where you are seen.

We are also reminded of the greatest friend—Jesus Christ. "No one has greater love than this, to lay down one's life for one's friends" (John 15:13). As the ultimate friend, Jesus cares about us so deeply that he gave his life on Calvary. His sacrificial love gives us a newness of life and the knowledge of what a true friend is.

I believe that in our hurry-up world, we diminish the value of a friend. If we've been betrayed or hurt by friends in the past, we may question the need for any. There are some women who, due to their demanding jobs or busy lifestyles, see friends as optional. If we have a car, there is no need to talk to people on the way to and from work. If we live alone, we have the Internet, television, and radio to entertain us. A substitute for friends can be our job, our hobbies, or even a pet. It can be easier to connect to an object or an animal than a person because people can betray, lie, and deceive.

Nevertheless, we still need friends or at least a friend in life. If not, a chronic loneliness can set in, and it can be detrimental. Research findings indicate that social support is a human necessity. People who are socially isolated, without meaningful relationships, are at increased risk for physical deterioration, mental illness, and even death. One expert has identified two types of loneliness. "There is emotional loneliness, which is about *quality* of contacts, not having a close, intimate relationship with one other person—in other words, being 'lonely in a crowd.' The only means by which this loneliness can be remedied is by finding another equally important relationship to fill the void, not just by becoming socially active in a superficial, nonintimate manner."[2]

"Social loneliness has to do with *quantity* of contacts: not having enough people or enough activity in one's life. Those relationships must include six elements if they are to be positive; a sense of security, social integration in a group setting, nurturing of some type (being cared for, affirmation), being made to feel of value, reliable systems (people you can count on and counsel), and guidance being offered.[3]

A woman can be surrounded by people, nevertheless, it is possible to be lonely in both ways. She can be socially lonely if she chooses not to talk with others or to participate in planned activities or if the activities are not meaningful to her. She can be emotionally lonely if all her contact with others is superficial.

People often find it hard to admit that they are lonely. Therefore, look for signs of social isolation within yourself, including the following:

- Aggression, anger
- Powerlessness, withdrawal from life
- Self-doubt, shame
- Confusion of past with present
- Feeling confined or deserted
- Difficulty setting goals and making decisions[4]

There are many images of friendships among African American women in the media that underscore the value and purpose of female friends. As we further examine the need for friends and single African American women, these are not overtly Christian images, but they are realistic and helpful. One such friendship was the familial relationship between Maxine, Regine, Sinclair, and Kadejah on the series *Living Single.*

These women were in their early twenties and shared a New York brownstone. They collectively learned about life and attempted to buffer the bumps and bruises that accompany growing pains. They served as family and security for each other. For example, if one of them was dating a guy who seemed suspect, the others sounded the alarm and he was dismissed. This family unit style of friendship offers the safety net that is needed. The friends offered parental, sibling, and extended family support. Sometimes you will need friends who offer a multitude of assistance.

There was a sounding board relationship between the characters Gina and Pam on the comedy *Martin*. The television series gave an accurate portrayal of a young woman loving an overbearing and exasperating boyfriend. Gina opted to concede and give in to the obnoxious Martin because she loved him. Her best friend Pam was her confidante and one of the few to stand up to Martin. Pam helped Gina make sense of her world. Sometimes you may need a friend to help you deal with your man or you may be the friend who helps her girlfriend deal with a difficult man.

The comedy of *Girlfriends* takes African American female friendships to a new level in the twenty-first century. These women demonstrate that friendships can be connections of diverse backgrounds and interests. Lynn, though highly degreed, was usually unemployed; Joan, a high-powered corporate attorney, is needy; Tonie, a real estate broker, has an overly inflated ego; Maya, Joan's secretary, does not have a college degree and is a single mom. This ensemble demonstrates that friends don't need to be mirrors of each other to sustain communion. In life, you can benefit from friends like these—friends who are at different stages of life and have contrasting personalities.

LEVELS OF FRIENDSHIPS

There are levels of friendships. There is the *best friend* who knows you like the back of her hand. You love your best friend and you would trust her with your life. Best friends have a proven track record that they support you in any and all situations. You can disagree with a best friend and still be friends. Then there are people whom you like, but you have determined that they will not get too close to you. They are valuable but perhaps due to distance or some annoying habit or time this person is not the closest to you. I call these people *just friends.*

The third category is *casual friends.* These people are fun to be with, and people whose company you enjoy. For example, they may be the people you spend time with at your son's baseball game. You do not share intimate, personal information; you do not rely on them or expect them to do something. *Acquaintances,* the fourth category, are people that you know only by name or by face. You may greet them but know nothing about them and they know nothing about you. An acquaintance may be someone at your bus stop or someone from the gym.

The vital role that friends play adjusts and adapts as they age. According to the book *Single in a Married World,* friendships can be traced throughout the life cycle. In their twenties, friends help singles carve out new identities, grow up, and successfully separate from their family. They teach what intimacy is without being married. In their thirties, friends add balance so that the focus for women isn't always about men. In their forties, friends provide companionship if a woman is not in a committed relationship. And after fifty, friendships provide a safety net to fend off the fear of finding oneself sick and alone.[5]

FRIENDSHIP AND MOTHERHOOD

Friendships can enhance your motherhood. Don't go it alone. If you are a single mom, your friends can help you keep all the balls in the air. It may be an extensive network of other moms with their cell numbers programmed into your phone, or just one reliable friend down the hall. If you unexpectedly have to work late and need someone to pick up your son from baseball practice, being able to pick up the phone and ask Camille to help you out is wonderful. Or being able to solicit advice from Sharon on how to make a butterfly costume for your daughter's play is great.

WORK FRIENDS

Friends are a necessity at work. Without them, the hours spent at the job would be unbearable. "Research shows that friends enhance your self-esteem and affect job satisfaction as well. They make your work life infinitely more pleasurable and relieve stress and even burnout."[6] Having someone to talk with at lunch or sit beside during group meetings is pleasant. Without friends, some people quit the job. "When people don't make friends on the job, they often wind up leaving."[7] "American employees now spend an average of forty-four hours a week on the job."[8] The queen knows how to make the most of those hours at work with savvy, sophisticated, and God-ordained wisdom.

"Friends are crucial to success in the corporate world. To advance in most organizations, you need the requisite skills to perform, but you also need relationships that have developed and nurtured in order to open doors, get things done, and deal with the bureaucracy."[9]

Friends at work are complicated because they are at the place of business and not the park. There is an expected level of conduct. Never be too relaxed or casual, because, after all, you are at work.

- Don't hang out or spend time lounging or pretending that you are at a party.
- Don't tell too much. The politics of an office or workplace are ever changing. The person that you told that you skip work to go to baseball games may be promoted to your supervisor or may be competing with you for advancement.
- Don't be surprised by betrayal. In the work world, there are no permanent friends or permanent enemies.
- Avoid office cliques. These cause needless office tension and can place you in a negative light if you are with the perceived "wrong" clique.
- Don't go to work to preach, teach, or evangelize in the break room. Your job is not your opportunity to broadcast your faith in the Lord. Placing a mammoth Bible on your desk and blasting gospel tunes on your office CD player are inappropriate office practices. Instead, let the light of Jesus emanate from your soul and lead people to Christ as they see him in you.
- Be leery of friendships with a subordinate or a superior. The differences between your work statuses could be problematic.

I like the advice given by Bishop T. D. Jakes about work. He said, "Don't go to work looking for friends, go to work to work."

As you become more and more queenlike, there will be reactions from your friends. Some may applaud, others may put you down. Debrena Jackson Gandy, author of *Sacred Pampering Principles,* advocates retraining family and friends. "There are certain tools and aids you can use to assist loved ones in their evolution as you move through your process. And it isn't just those inside the home who can be affected by your 'adjustments'; it can also be people outside your home who have grown accustomed to a certain you and may offer some resistance. This includes relatives, co-workers, neighbors, friends, church members, or a boss or supervisor."[10]

MARRIED FRIENDS

Married women and single women can and should be friends. The institution of marriage does not suddenly end the friendship. A divorce should not cancel out the bond that held you two together. Of course, there are horror stories of best friends being torn asunder because of a marriage or a divorce. Some say that the two should not mix because you have nothing in common anymore. Others say that your contrasting lifestyles are bound to cause friction. But don't let that happen to you and your married best buddy. Once you find yourself in this situation, sit down with your friend and talk about going forward with new parameters of the relationship. I've provided ten tips to help you maintain a healthy relationship with her.

1. Be aware of real and often intense emotions about your relationship. If your best single girlfriend gets married, you may feel abandoned or less important in her eyes.
2. The single friend may erroneously consider the married friend to have a perfect life because she has a man and money. This could be totally false. Perception is not necessarily reality.
3. Single friends should not overutilize their married friends with favors such as watching her kids, or hookups with one of her husband's friends. Those requests will wear thin if repetitious and have little bearing on the true nature of the friendship.
4. Beware of resentment of her marital status. When you go home alone and she goes home to a house full of kids and a spouse, you may ask, "Why her and not me?" Don't be surprised if she is not asking herself the same question as she longs for the solitude that you have.

5. Understand that girlfriend-time is probably limited. The two of you cannot talk on the phone for hours or hang out at your favorite spots till the wee hours anymore. The shopping and spending may change also. Accept the changes and go with the flow.
6. Be aware that her husband or your boyfriend may be jealous of your relationship. The girlfriend-time that the two of you share may seem threatening to him, especially if you've know her longer than you've known him. Sometimes, inviting him on an outing with you can calm these insecurities.
7. A worse case scenario is when your married girlfriend's husband makes a pass at you. This dilemma can have catastrophic implications on your relationship. The big issue is do you tell her or not?
8. Establish boundaries in the relationship. There must be areas that are off-limits in your relationship. Those areas are the details of her marriage and the details of you and your man. Those intimate details must remain between the two of them, whether it is their sexual preferences or what they argued about last night.
9. Don't hate their marriages, their ability to maintain intimacy, or their ability to conceive. Rather, appreciate what God is doing in their lives and know that it is no secret what God can do: what God has done for others, God can do for you.
10. Pray for her and her marriage. Ask God to give her and her spouse a union that is covered in 1 Corinthians 13:4–13 love.

Here is a letter from a single woman who has the blues because of a married best friend:

Dear Dr. Patterson,

I am a single woman with a problem with my married friend. Keisha has been my best friend since the third grade. We have done everything together since then. We were cheerleaders to-

gether in high school and were roommates in college. She is my sister, even though I have blood sisters too. Keisha married a guy that I did not know about a year ago. I did not particularly care for him, but it was her choice. I went by her house to drop something off; she was not there, but her husband was. Much to my surprise he hugged me, grabbed my butt, and tried to get me to have sex with him! I was stunned. I ran out of the house and have been avoiding Keisha because I do not know what to do. Help!

Groped and Confused

Dear Groped and Confused,

You are in a major dilemma between a married friend and a single friend. It was not your fault. You have done nothing wrong. If you tell Keisha what happened, she might not believe it was her husband's idea. If you don't tell her, the husband may tell her it was your idea. Your best option is to tell her immediately and let her handle it her way. The consequences will be out of your hands.

CHURCH FRIENDS

Church friends are people with whom you share a special Christian experience of worship and serving God. They are your colaborers in the vineyard and are very special people, as they may nurture your Christian journey or you may help them on theirs. You may sing together in the choir or serve together on the diaconate board. The bond of church membership draws you together and keeps your relationship strong. Most of your activities with church friends may center around the church and may not have the same allure as those with nonchurch friends. The closeness can be problematic, as one caller explained.

Dear Dr. Patterson,

I have a friend at church that seems to overspiritualize everything from the weather to what type of seasoning that is on the food. It's always having to do with God's will or the power of the Holy Ghost. I am a believer, but I believe she is taking it too far and getting on my last Christian nerve. Should I end our friendship and if so, how do I do this at a small church?

Perplexed

Dear Perplexed,

Your friend is one who acknowledges God at all times in a tangible way. She needs an immediate connection between everything and God. She is not comfortable without God's presence in every sentence that she makes. There are plenty of people like her. The problems is that they expect everyone to act like them. All of us do not need an immediate connection between everything and God. We have the confidence and faith that God is there and at work. People like your friend can be dogmatic in their beliefs and wind up getting on the nerves of other people. Her habit will more than likely not change. So don't try and change her. You will have to make a drastic decision; whether to end your association or remain with her. Being a part of a small church will make the separation more difficult to carry out. I suggest that you broaden your circle of friends at the church to include other women like yourself. The more new friends that you bring into the circle, the easier it may be to either tolerate her or ease out of the circle. The bottom line is that a friend should not be someone who irritates us.

FRIENDS ONLINE

Online, friends may break the boredom and attract women around a common topic. Chat rooms give women the much-needed chance to express themselves and be heard. Online friends are a convenience of this high-tech- society. We can create a virtual community with a computer without ever uttering a word or leaving the house.

Jackie has a circle of friends online. Through the Internet, she entered a network of women who gladly understands and hears her concerns. "I have never met these women, probably never will, but they are my family. They know more about what is going on with me than my real family," she said. "I log on the first thing in the morning and check in all day from work. Of course, there are nighttime check-ins too." This is her cyber family and it is helpful to her. These friendships work because they may connect women who live in isolated cities or have demanding jobs.

There are downsides with online friends that may happen if we withdraw from seeing and communicating with family and friends in person. There is the fantasy that Internet friends care more than in-person friends, when in reality, this is a group of strangers united around a computer terminal. Further, addictions can occur. "The Internet—like food or drugs in other addictions—provides the 'high' and addicts become dependent on this cyberspace high to feel normal. They substitute unhealthy relationships for healthy ones." Estimates suggest that 5 to 10 percent of the population suffer from Internet addiction.[11]

HOW TO BE A GOOD FRIEND

If you want to have friends, you must be friend-worthy. The scriptures tell us that those who would have a friend, would first be friendly. Are you having trouble making friends or keeping friends? Be sure and review chapter 5, "What's Really Bothering You?" Consider that the problem may not be them; maybe it's you. Incidents from our childhoods can impact the way we make friends and the type of friends that we are. Parents who were very critical or emotionally absent, for example, influence our ability to be a friend. One expert tells us that we "are often drawn to people who treat us the way we expect. Someone sensitive to criticism may unconsciously pick critical people as friends. Someone mistrustful may choose selfish people who are likely to hurt her. A 'doormat' often chases a controlling person. We're attracted to people who push our sensitive buttons because they're familiar—similar to our parents, siblings, or others of significance in our childhood."[12]

One radio caller asked this question:

Dear Dr. Patterson,

This may seem shallow but I have a problem. I have a girlfriend that I work with and we go to lunch together sometimes, to church, and to plays. My issue is that we exchange gifts for Christmas and birthdays, and I usually spend at least $25.00 or more for her gifts. But I noticed that the gifts she gives to me seem cheaper. I say this because she left the price tag on the gift she gave me for my birthday. It was $7.99. The only reason that I bring this up is because we are supposed to be good friends, and last Saturday we went shopping together to buy a baby shower gift for another friend of ours and she spent over $40.00 for her gift. I know that I sound shallow, but my feelings are hurt. What should I do?

Hurt Giver

Dear Hurt Giver,

Your friend has a different concept of gifts than you do. You could not and should not change that. Your gifts to her should not be given in hopes of getting something in the same price range. To alleviate your pain, I suggest that you lower the price of her gifts. Then the two of you will be equal and you can stop worrying about the price.

If you have good friends, hold on to them with these tips.

- Be considerate. You should keep their feelings in mind at all times. This friendship is not only about you, it's about them.
- Be conscious of their needs too. Don't dominate the conversations with all of your problems and concerns. Let them share too.
- Be a listener. Your friends should consider you a shoulder to cry on when times get rough.
- Be a giver and be generous. Remember birthdays, holidays with gifts, celebrations, and tokens.
- Don't be judgmental. When friends share issues, don't condemn them and sentence them to punishment.
- Keep confidences. Whatever your friend tells you must remain with you. She is trusting you to keep her matters between the two of you.

Author Jan Yager offers a helpful checklist when looking for a new good friend. I like her approach because it does not rush into friends, it is slow and methodical. Over time, the person needs to rise from an acquaintance to the level of a good friend through tangible acts. She offers no guarantees or sure predictors, just a means of identifying potentially red flags.

- Does your acquaintance always tell the truth?
- Does your acquaintance treat coworkers, subordinates or superiors, family members, or romantic partners in a respectful, reliable, and polite way?
- If this acquaintance reminds you of someone from your past or present, is it someone you liked, admired, and respected?
- Are you impressed by the loyalty and quality of the other friends of this new acquaintance?

- Do you find yourself looking forward to seeing your acquaintance again, or to receiving the next e-mail, or the next phone call?
- Have you gotten verbal or nonverbal signs from your acquaintance that she wants to become your friend?[13]

I pray that this chapter has helped you focus frankly on friendships and that you are now prepared to develop and maintain positive relationships with female friends.

QUESTIONS FOR REFLECTION

1. Do your friends help or harm your title as queen?
2. Why are friends needed in your life?
3. How does the Bible speak to you about friends?
4. Are you tired of, angry with, or alienated from other women?
5. Have you been hurt or betrayed by a female?
6. Do you need to polish your friend-making skills?

PRAYER

God of Connections, I understand that friends are a gift from you. Give me a spirit of friendliness that I may attract and maintain healthy friendships. Deliver me from a spirit of loneliness. Open my eyes to the potential friends all around me and lead me in the productive pathways. Empower me to be a good friend. Amen.

8 · REACH OUT INSTEAD OF LASH OUT

I see a devisive wall separating men and women. Stereotypes, anger, and misunderstanding comprise the wall. It's kept us at each other's throats long enough. The ability to connect is crucial because in our community there is a legacy of chaos. This troubles me so much. Twenty years ago when I penned my first book for singles, I quoted relationship expert duo Nathan and Julia Hare, who delivered the bad news that we do not get along. They said

> If we had to name the most tragic failure of Black people historically in the United States, we'd have to point to the relations between Black males and Black females. Our confusion or negligence in this area is both curious and shocking, because the relationships between male and female are the most basic of all human entanglements and the most crucial for the subjugation of a people.[1]

Now ten years later, it seems that not much has changed. As I remain on the battlefield fighting for happy, whole relationships, I feel overwhelmed and understocked with ammunition. I am inviting you to join my team. We are a team of positive relationships and what we do is give single women hope that they can have a healthy, positive relationship. We dispel the rumor that there aren't any more good men left.

Let's take down the wall. We can do that with educated minds, willing spirits, and good attitudes. Queen, there are good men all around us. There are good men at church, men at work, men in the neighborhood, and more. A queen must not only understand them, she also must have the ability to relate to them. The ability to relate is crucial because, in our community, there is a legacy of poor relationships.

In this chapter, we will reach out to men, hear their stories, and learn to relate to them. First, we will examine the process of meeting a man. There is more to say than space in which to say it. We'll answer the age-old question, "Should a woman approach a man?" Then, we will look at an old-fashioned way of dating—a blind date—and also a newfangled way—Internet dating. Next we will look into the hearts of men and allow them to speak to us about their concerns. I will introduce you to five great guys who were a part of my reality program. As part of a ministry to help women understand men, they have opened up their hearts. Finally, we will close with a few of the most interesting dating dilemmas that occurred on the radio broadcast.

Before we go any further, let's spend time around the ever-popular belief that women can't approach men. In churches, when the topic of women approaching men is raised, a chorus of disdain is heard. A text in Proverbs is used like a billy club to beat down assertive sisters. This fervent belief is based on a commonly held interpretation of Proverbs 18:22, which says, "He who finds a wife finds a good thing and obtains favor from God." The text endorses marriage and encourages single men to seek wives and settle down.

The text is also instructing them to have high standards and prefer women who are "wife material." The text also alludes to a degree of difficulty in securing such a woman. He will have to find or search for her, but it will be worth the search.

This text is not saying that a woman should not seek a man who is husband material too. It addresses the conduct of men. Please bear in mind that in the Old Testament world, women were considered as their husbands' possessions—like cows and horses. A woman had no voice, power, or influence. It was natural that a woman would remain silent until she was picked by a man for marriage. An example of this is found in Genesis 29:18 when Jacob selected Rachel for his wife and bartered the engagement through her father.

It should be noted that there is a biblical example of a woman finding a husband and this union being blessed by God. In the book of Ruth, at the end of harvest, Naomi devised a plan. She advised Ruth to wash, and go down to the threshing floor. Marking where Boaz lay down after eating and drinking, Ruth was to join him and uncover his feet—a euphemism for genitals (Ruth 3:3–4)[2] The plan to meet a man was fruitful. Boaz noticed her and soon they married. Their union was blessed; evidence is that Jesus Christ was a descendant.

This does not mean that women should aggressively hound men, call them incessantly, and beg them for dates. This says that if a woman sees a man that she likes, she can say hello, or start a conversation, or even give him her business card. It is incorrect to think of an image of a woman plastered against a wall waiting for a man to approach her and pick her.

Blind dates may be arranged or set up by well-meaning family and friends. They are hated by some and requested by others. It depends heavily on who is doing the arranging. If you have a well-connected person who sets up dates for you, this could be a positive arrangement for meeting great guys. Even if the arranger is not so great, don't rule out the possibility of meeting a keeper. Your attitude determines it all on a blind date.

Here are a few pointers:

- Get a good attitude. You might not have one, but get one. This attitude should be based on your hopes for a fun date. You can set the tone for disaster or a memorable date.
- Select a fun location. If your surroundings are enjoyable, they can compensate for a not-so-enjoyable date. And if he flops, at least you can talk about where you were.
- Prepare to talk. Blind dates are about getting to know someone you've never met. You will be expected to communicate about yourself. Have funny stories prepared and interesting tidbits to share about yourself.
- Don't be childish. It is tempting to have friends follow you on the date and intervene if need be. It makes you look juvenile if your buddies tag along with you wherever you go.
- If the situation is not working and you do not connect with the guy say so in a gentle way. It's better than lying to him and dodging his calls for a month. At the end of the date say something like, "Hey I had a nice time. It was good of Jack to bring us together. But I don't think we are a match."

ONLINE DATING

Interested in meeting a man online? I don't think it's a sin, or wrong to do so. I see it as an extension of our high-tech world that believers can use to their benefit. Join the other "forty-five million people who have visited as many as 2,500 matchmaking sites on the Internet."[3] "Nearly six million Americans have used the Internet to find a mate. But 75 percent of online relationships never reach the point of in-person dating."[4]

Carol dates online all the time. "It's a lot more convenient for me to meet guys on the Internet. There are a lot of safe, fun chat rooms where I go to talk and meet people. No, I have not met the man of my dreams yet. But I believe he is out there. There is only one problem; my church family would kill me if they knew. They are really against anything like this. They believe that the Internet is of the devil, so I have to get on the devil by myself."

Single sister Cheryl Green, author of *World Wide Search, the Savvy Christian's Guide to Online Dating,* offers a host of tips to ensure that your Internet experience is positive. She writes, "I am a Christian single on the same journey you are making. Although I am not married yet, I have dated several Christian men I met online. I have also made scores of friends from all over the world."[5] Due to her wealth of experience, Cheryl outlines the advantages and disadvantages of dating online.

Advantages of Online Dating

- You don't have to rush. You can control the pace of the conversation or take your time and answer questions thoughtfully.
- You don't feel pressured. You can concentrate on communication without the distractions of what you'll wear.
- There is time to reflect and gain perspective. You can save your e-mail conversations and reread them later.
- You have access to an incredible number of singles. No longer are you limited to meeting others only in your own city or region.

Disadvantages of Online Dating

- You can't see the other person. You miss out on the nuances, since written words leave out much of the information that is communicated in spoken words.
- You might be tempted to read into a message. When you rely on text-only communication, it's easy to hear what you want to hear.
- You may fall victim to romantic fantasies. Online communication often frees people to present themselves as wittier, more outgoing, or more creative than they really are in person.

- You'll encounter widely contrasting backgrounds and experiences. Since the Internet expands the universe of available singles, it's likely that you and your match will share very little common history.[6]

One caller asked an interesting Internet dating question:

Dear Dr. Pattterson,

I broke up with a man in 1998 after a four-year relationship. He moved out of town for his job a few months after we broke up and we lost contact with each other. He called me during the Christmas holidays and we have been talking a lot since then. He is going to move back to town soon and he told me that he wants me to consider getting back with him. This is the man that I thought I would marry and it seems like God has put him back in my life. The only problem is that since the last time he saw me I have gone from 140 lbs to 250. He asked me to send a photo of myself via the Internet before our meeting so he can focus on my beauty. I emailed him an old photo of a slimmer me. I don't want him to see me like this, but I do need to be honest. What should I do?

A Little Heavy

Dear A Little Heavy,

You'd better be honest with this man before he gets to town or there just may be some trouble. I advise you to get on the Internet and send him a current photo. If your weight is going to be an issue, let it be an issue long distance. Think of the shocked expression on his face if he were unaware of your size. If he is truly into you, the size won't matter. If he is not, he will keep on stepping.

The journey from meeting a man to determining if you will date this man should be taken at God's pace, not yours. Take the time to ask God first, should I go out with him? Only God has the answers. Yes, he may be fine, but is fine enough? I love the advice found in the Song of Solomon, "I adjure you, O daughters of Jerusalem, do not stir up or awaken love before it is ready" (Song of Solomon 8:4). That means, take it slow. Pray and ask God for guidance.

A MAN'S PERSPECTIVE

In this book, we looked at our pain extensively. Have you ever wondered about the pain a man feels?

Terrence puts up a good front in public, but he has not gotten over Sharmaine. "She was my first true love. I loved her from the moment that I saw her at church. When I entered the fellowship hall of the church, my eyes made a beeline in her direction. Sister girl was beautiful, thick, and fine. She was enjoying the delicious foods at a reception and even though I was fasting, I ate some too, just to be around her. I kept seeing her around the church and one day I approached her for a conversation. I asked for her phone number, and when I called, we talked for hours. I declare that I had met my soul mate.

"I invested time and money to make our first date special. When I picked her up, the first thing she did was get in the car and get on her cell phone. After a ten-minue conversation with a girlfriend, she began to talk to me. We went to the park, a romantic restaurant for dinner, and then a carriage ride. It was better than good. We made plans to get together the next day. But I found out that I had to work and called her. That was when I saw a side of her that scared me. She became verbally abusive. She cussed me up and down—over that?"

"But the girl was fine so I overlooked it. The more I dated her, the more that anger would surface. It came out over little things, like my driving or the color shirt I had on. Pretty soon I was scared to say anything because it might set her off. The last straw was when she pulled a knife on me. I did not believe that this fine sister had a knife in her purse. She just lost it one night and threatened to cut me. You know what? I don't need a wacky woman like that, no matter how fine she is or whether she is my soul mate or not!"

Mark Crutcher, author of the book *Checkmate*, shares that the pain he feels is actually the seeds that he sowed.

> For the first time in my life, I understand the pain that I have heard many women express. Pain they have endured after encounters with men who have loved them and left them. I can identify with the confusion caused by not knowing what I had done wrong; crying until there are no tears left; and days that turn into weeks of sleepless pain. You know the type—a ladies' man, a player, a pimp, the man with all the right moves.
>
> "For about 14 years, I engaged in a game not unlike the game of chess. In a chess match, the objective is to place the opponent's king in an inescapable position on the game board. In the game I played, my objective was to persuade women to maintain casual, uncommitted, sexual relationships with me. By the time they realized that my intentions were purely physical, it was too late. They were already addicted to the experiences we shared and could not or would not let go. Checkmate.
>
> "It was a sad day a couple of years ago [when] I realized the tables could turn and had turned. You see the woman I loved walked out of my life without any warning . . . on a fall afternoon, I stood proudly wearing a white tuxedo, in the presence of family and friends, waiting for the music to begin and her to walk down the aisle. The music played, everyone smiled, and waited anxiously, but she never showed.[7]

In my quest to help good people find great relationships, I produced a reality television program called *Mission Get Married.* The goal was not to get everyone married, rather to teach the basics of a sound relationship. If it grew into marriage, great. If not, great also.

There were five extraordinary men in the cast. Let me introduce them. Duran was a thirty-four-year-old computer analyst with an engaging smile and lots of charisma. Donald was a forty-nine-year-old radio personality. As the elder statesman of the group, he shared a seasoned perspective that was needed. Curtis was a thirty-three-year-old computer technician who had been bruised by love and needed restoration. Marlon was a thirty-one-year-old owner of a construction company. His smooth persona had all the ladies hanging on every word. Daryl was a thirty-nine-year-old attorney who opened himself up for restructuring from head to toe.

Each of the guys was looking for love and they were willing to spend a few months with me in pastoral counseling and public seminars to help them become the right person that they might find the right person. They had their own set of luggage, as we all do. The difference was that they did not mind sharing theirs.

Curtis sometimes put up a wall to protect himself. Marlon was too critical of women and wanted them to be perfect. Donald admitted that he was set in his ways, which could block a potentially great relationship. Daryl tended to overanalyze his relationships. He almost put the woman on trial as if he was in the courtroom. Duran had pain behind that smile. His laughter covered up issues that needed to be dealt with.

These five guys showed us that men seeking love is a beautiful and sometimes entertaining thing. Have you ever wondered what goes on in a man's world of relationships? I've compiled a few of the most vital conversations from the radio broadcast.

There Is Pressure to Conform to Stereotypes

"I am a thirty-four-year-old single black male. I started a new job in March, and because of my job pace, I pretty much keep to myself and concentrate on doing my job. I do speak to people that I work with, but have not started any friendships. There are a lot of females in my workplace that I have noticed do a lot of non-work-related talking. I have been asked by a couple of women if I have a wife or girlfriend and I have told them no. The other day, I was at my desk and one of the young ladies came into my area and asked me why I had no pictures of anyone on my desk and several other personal questions. I told her that I did not think that she needed to know. She said that I must be one of those down low brothers that Oprah was talking about. Now there is a rumor out at the office that says I am gay. Why is it that when a man is about business and is not hounding, he 'has' to be gay?"

Am I Wrong for Dating Three Different Women?

"I am a twenty-four-year-old single Christian man who loves God! I am not involved in any type of serious relationships. I have three young ladies that I currently see. We go to movies, out to eat, enjoy bowling and things like that, but there is nothing serious or physical, not even kissing. We are just friends. They all know that I am not interested in a serious relationship right now, and they go out with other people too. I was talking with a brother at my church and he was telling me that I was wrong for going out with three different ladies because it sends the message that I am a playa. This is not the case."

Singles Ministry Creates a Mauling

"I am a thirty-three-year-old single man who is an active member of a great church that offers programming to meet all my needs. There are lots of people here my age, so what is there to complain about? There is one ministry that I want to participate in, the singles ministry, but I can't because the women are too fierce. They out-number the men six-to-one and it can sometimes look like a feeding frenzy instead of a church ministry.

"If there is a discussion time, the women shout and loud talk the men. And if they are not being rude, they are all up on the men trying to get a date. The singles pastor is trying to keep the peace, but things have gotten out of control. I want to be fed by the ministry, but I can't stand the atmosphere."

QUESTIONS FOR REFLECTION

1. Why do you think African American men and women struggle to form healthy relationships?
2. What is your interpretation of Proverbs 18:22?
3. Why do some women avoid blind dates? What about you?
4. Would you consider Internet dating? Why or why not?
5. After reading the section about men and their pain, what is your reaction?

PRAYER

God of Relationships, I want positive connections with men. Please free me from needless anger and fear. Give me a renewed understanding of men that I may be able to tear down the walls that divide us. Amen.

9 · DEFINE, DON'T CONFINE, THE MEN IN YOUR LIFE

A queen knows a king when she sees one. We must have a built-in detection system. A king is a good man. A good man can be short, tall, thick, or thin. A good man can drive a truck or drive homeruns across the baseball diamond. A good man can have a Ph.D. or no degree at all. What makes him a good man is the way he carries and conducts himself, and how he treats you.

In the Bible, there are a host of good men. One that stands out in relation to a single woman is Joseph in the New Testament. Joseph stood by his woman in her greatest hour of need. Men who will not abandon us when we are hurting are good men. After a conversation with the angel of God, he stayed with Mary even though she was pregnant with a child other than his. "Joseph, son of David, do not be afraid to take Mary as your wife, for the child conceived in her is from the Holy Spirit" (Matt. 1:20).

It is vital that we are able to look beyond the exterior of the man to the heart of a man. There we can see what's truly going on in his life and gain insight into his context. African American men have had, and still do have, numerous challenges. Their context can be dire and depressing. We delineated the challenges we face in chapter 5, and our men have their share and more. We benefit from an understanding of their situation. No discussion about men would be complete without first laying all the facts on the table. From the single woman's perspective, the number of available men is crucial. The pool of marriageable black men appears to get smaller every year.

> A traditional requisite for marriage has been having a steady job or the prospect of one. This status has not been readily achieved given the current unemployment rates. At the time of this writing, over half a million black men are in jails or prisons, and as many more could be sent or returned there if they violate their parole or probation. And perhaps as many as a million more have records as felons. . . . Another large group is debilitated by drugs and alcohol or mental illness. In addition, the death rates for younger men have reached terrifying levels. In the fifteen to twenty-five age group, the mortality rate for black men is now 3.25 times that for black women, with the principal cause of being gunned down by a member of their own race."[1]

Have you spent time with a good man? As I hear more and more of our stories, I am learning that some of us never have. One woman shared with me that because she never had a good man, she put negative things in his place.

"Although I have never been married, I have always had a deep desire to be married. I enjoy companionship, and I love doing things with people. I guess you would categorize me as an outgoing person. In fact, most of my friends feel that I am much too busy to have a man in my life. Yet, I do believe that the right man would make me slow down. I have to admit, as I am getting older, the desire to have a soul mate and a lifelong companion is growing stronger in my spirit. As I look over my life, I can't say that I have ever had a really good relationship with a male. Unfortunately, I have learned the hard way what

I don't want in a relationship. But what I do want is unconditional love; because that is the one thing I do have to give. My true desire is to recognize someone who is capable of treating me the way that I deserve to be treated. At this point in my life I refuse to accept anything less.

"I know in the early years, I associated love with sex. I was looking for love in all the wrong places, and I found myself trying to fill in a lot of empty spaces that were left in my heart. However, after I developed a strong relationship with the Lord, He filled that void. I have been celibate for a number of years, and I truly believe that sex is only sanctioned in marriage. Trust me, my abstinence has helped me weed out a lot of people. I do believe that God does have that special person for me. However, if He doesn't, I have learned to celebrate myself, and I will continue to enjoy life and capture every moment that God presents to me."

Let's be honest. Some of the guys that we have spent time with over the years don't qualify for the title of good men. This occurs because we lack a clear understanding of what a good man is. We are operating on flawed information. If you don't know what a man is, you will have tremendous difficulty navigating the waters of relationships. You may be looking for something that does not exist. Or you may be burdened with unrealistic expectations that may never be met.

In this chapter, you will be given the tools to define men and understand them. The alternative is to confine or limit them to erroneous lists, lost places, lies, and lust. After reading this chapter, you will have a queen's perspective on men. You will learn to understand and appreciate the gender differences. You will determine if you are a basher or a booster of men, and how to become a booster if you are a basher. You will learn how to appreciate the value of a platonic friend and what types of men to avoid.

To gain accurate information, let's hear from men about men. I've assembled a panel of articulate, nationally known men who write about love. They are William July, author of *Understanding the Tin Man,* and Ron Elmore, author of *How to Love a Black Man.* There's one more that must be added because he has truly articulated the differences between men and women—John Gray. His book *Men Are from Mars, Women Are from Venus* is priceless.

Men and women are not the same. Different does not mean better than or worse than. Different means that men and women don't think or act the same. I believe that our differences are great, but I did not feel this way until I understood them. Before then I was confused and angry sometimes. The differences make life very exciting, unless you don't understand what the differences are. First and foremost, remember that God made Adam and Eve, male and female, man and woman. Even though God created us both, in God's image we are not the same, we are opposites. A source of the trouble is that we have not cultivated an appreciation for our differences and often we attempt to treat men like we treat women. Let him be a man. You be a woman and celebrate the contrasts.

John Gray offers insight into the differences that men and women have communicating with each other. According to Gray, women talk to figure things out, and men go into caves or pull away emotionally to figure things out. Men don't seek to slight women, but it gives the men the privacy they need to process the information alone. Once they are done, they come out of their caves or their time of silence and are interactive again.

John Gray wrote, "Women have a lot to learn about men before their relationships can be really fulfilling. They need to learn that when a man is upset or stressed out he will automatically stop talking and go into his cave to work things out. They need to learn that no one is allowed in that cave, not even the man's best friends."[2]

Does this help you understand what is going on with men any better? If we are going into his cave, following him because he won't answer our questions, this may explain why. Or if we are wondering why our man will not talk his problems through with us, maybe he is still in his cave.

One listener asked, "Dr. Patterson: My fiancé does not talk much. In fact I do most of the talking when we are together. He does not seem to mind, but it bothers me a lot. What should I do?"

I responded, "You are about to marry a quiet man and you may want to get an idea of what he is thinking before you go any further. His silence may mean he is content with the situation or he is scared and does not know how to escape. It must be frustrating not to know his thoughts. Be sure that you can accept his silence. It probably will not change once you marry."

Understanding men also means learning their language. It is not like ours. Until you master it, you will be confused and confounded. Here are a few examples. When a man says, "I am not ready for a relationship," this really means, "I am not ready for a relationship, but I'll have sex with you." "I haven't met the right woman yet" really means "I don't know what I am looking for in a woman." "I am confused right now" really means "I'm confused and I'll probably hurt you."[3]

The area of sex is another contrast between men and women. A survey entitled *Sex in America: The Definitive Study* revealed that African American men and women differ greatly in their attitudes toward sex.

> The survey included a section in which sexual attitudes were categorized as traditional, relational, and recreational. The traditional category represented persons who stated that their sexual behavior is always guided by religious beliefs. The relational category represented persons who believed that sex should be a part of a loving relationship, but not necessarily reserved for marriage. The recreational category represented persons who believed that sex need not have anything to do with love."[4]

Black males numbered 42.3 percent of the recreational category, as compared to 8.9 percent of black women. In the relational category black males numbered 25.4 percent, black females 45.8 percent. Finally, black males numbered 32.3 percent in the traditional category, and black females numbered 45.3 percent.[5] These statistical contrasts explain why we are often at wits end when sexually involved with men. Obviously we approach the issue differently than they do.

Despite the differences, a queen is not intimidated or overwhelmed by men. In fact, she enjoys their company. A woman who is the exact opposite of this is known as a basher. She bashes men by putting them down to make herself feel good. Male bashing is popular in some circles because the sisters have had rough relationship experiences. We've probably bashed before and it felt good to vent, even though we knew it was wrong. "Bashers are women who expect Black men to be pitiful, and who take responsibility for pointing out their flaws to them and making them pay for them."[6] Dr. Ron Elmore offers the psychology behind this behavior when he writes, "Bashing has great appeal because it has anger and indignation at its core. Anger feels very powerful—especially when you feel very weak. Lashing out, setting straight, or paying back a Black man can help you forget that your heart was vulnerable to him in the first place. When you are angry you feel strong and therefore safe."[7]

Take this test to see if you are a basher:

- You get a secret jolt of satisfaction when another woman agrees with your sharp criticism of a black man or laughs at your disparaging remarks.
- There is a particular black man whom you believe has owed you an apology for some time.
- You sometimes daydream about conflicting situations where you are successful in putting a man "in his place."
- A number of times men have told you "lighten up" or "give me a break" or "chill out" in response to your style of relating to them.

Instead, proudly be a booster, a woman who builds men up. She is not weak-minded or gullible. Take this test to see if you are a booster:

- You get a personal sense of joy when you see a brother doing well.
- You have forgiven the wayward men in your life and moved on.

- You sometimes daydream about an old boyfriend and how you'd like to thank him for the lessons your relationship taught you about you.
- A number of times men have thanked you for your positive words and encouragement.
- You see a man down on his luck as struggling, not sorry.

MALE PLATONIC FRIENDS

Do platonic friends exist? Yes, men and women can be friends and not lovers. *JET* magazine once asked my opinion of the question; can men and women just be friends? I said, "Yes, they can and should be." It is a wonderful thing to have a best friend who is man. The opposite sex can bring a new dimension to the friendship. They give us valued information on men. I caught a lot of flack for my pro-platonic remarks, and it surprised me. Many people resist the idea that a single man and a single woman can truly just be friends without any romantic attachment. It is assumed that sex will creep into the relationship at some point. It is a great tragedy that male-female relationships have sunk to this depth. Godly men and women should be able to enjoy the relationship of brother and sister in Christ. I enjoy platonic relationships with men that have nothing to do with sex or romance and have everything to do with common interests. Platonic friends are very valuable to a single woman. They give her a contrasting perspective on men and allow her to try new thoughts and ideas on the opposite sex without penalty.

Admittedly, things can go awry. One woman called with an interesting problem. "I have a platonic friend and we have been the best of friends for ten years. We met in college and have kept in touch ever since. We go to lunch, dinner, movies, sporting events and more. We are like brother and sister. I enjoy it but my friends at church keep insisting that there is more to it. I get angry and I say no. What's the problem? Well, after ten years what they say is true. I am starting to fall for him. What should I do? Tell him and potentially ruin a great platonic relationship or keep quiet and hold my feelings of love to myself?"

I responded, "If you are feeling this way, chances are he may be also. The two of you may be able to make that uncommon transition from platonic to romantic. Yet there is a great risk also. He may not share your feelings and it may be very embarrassing if he does not reciprocate. Will you be able to save face? Before you share your feelings, pray and give it a little more time. This is nothing to rush into. It's been ten years, so he is not going anywhere."

While platonic relationships are very valuable to a single woman, they should be approached carefully. Here are tips for not blowing it:

- Beware of your emotional state. The longing for companionship can distort the true nature of the relationship. If you are hungry for attention and affection, you may overwhelm the platonic male who reaches out to you.
- Platonic relationships should be tailored to the appropriate age and stage of the man and the woman. The type of relationship you would have while you are single and twenty-one would be a different type of platonic relationship to be held at forty-five, single, with three kids.
- Always monitor the motivations. Why are you doing this and what are you getting out of it? Ensure that you are not being used, throwing away valuable time, or being betrayed. Keep prayer a central part of the relationship and seek God's face for guidance.
- Do not allow a platonic friend to interfere with a potential husband. In a worst case scenario, the platonic friend could become territorial and scare away the prospective spouse. Keep your boundaries in place; reserve your emotional intimacy for the boyfriend, not the platonic friends.

OFFICE ROMANCE

A queen values her employment and does not risk it by foolishly intertwining love with work. Trying to court and get your job done is too much to deal with. Emotions can get out of control, and you can find yourself out of a job. However, if love at work sounds good let me offer some pointers. One caller had a pressing question on the issue.

Dear Dr. Patterson,

I know a minister at work who has been pursuing me sexually for a few months now. He once worked in the same office as me. To make a long story short, I gave in and now that I have done it, I feel really, really bad. If approached again, what should be my stance?

Confused Worker

Dear Confused Worker,

The office and romance makes for a dangerous combination. This minister who is pursuing you is way out of line, but obviously he was successful at his office goal. I suggest that you put as much distance between the two of you as possible. When you see him, tell him that the sex was a mistake and it will not happen again. Keep your mind on your job and don't allow any worries about him to distract you. If need be, ask to be transferred somewhere else.

Perhaps your office romance turned out better than hers. Such relationships can start off wonderful and end up wicked. The sweet guy in the cubicle next to you seemed so cute. Plus he was convenient. He liked you and you liked him. Coming to work was a joy. But after a quick three weeks of romantic e-mails and kisses in the break room he suddenly went cold. The office grapevine says he's now cuddling with another cutie on the thirty-seventh floor. Now that cubicle is too close. You are forced to look at him and hear him constantly during the day. Work is the worst place to be.

You've got to learn the rules of romance while at work before you jump in. It is treacherous, and depending on your office, it could be illegal. While an office romance with one of your peers is tricky, you should never date above or below your rank at the office. Sure the guy who delivers the mail is cute, but he is off limits. So is the CEO who directs all the people in the building. Human resources professionals universally say supervisor/subordinate relationships court disaster. Here's how some companies handle this.

"If a boss and an underling start a fling, companies are wise to move the underling to a different boss—a tough proposition for smaller companies. As coworkers continue to find dates and soul mates at the office, employers increasingly are asking amorous employees to sign forms acknowledging that the relationships are consensual. Office romances can cost companies more than the productivity lost to flirtatious e-mails. Rare a decade ago, so-called love contracts are becoming standard in human resources arsenals. Such contracts can shield an innocent employee from false accusations of a scorned coworker and protect employers from pricey sexual harassment lawsuits if a romance implodes. The documents are written proof that a company is trying to provide a hostile-free work environment. One form runs five pages and includes prohibitions such as holding hands or touching in an affectionate or sexually suggestive manner.[9]

Following are helpful rules of engagement in the workplace:

- Never date down. Don't get involved with a subordinate. You open the company to a sexual harassment claim if things go sour. It can hurt morale. Employees can say they were denied promotion because they weren't dating the boss.
- Never date up. If your boss hits on you, request that he or she check with human resources to see if that's allowed.
- Look outside the box. If you must date someone from work, it's better if that person is far removed from your area. There will be fewer chances to interact and embarrass yourself.

- Avoid PDAs. Public displays of affection are a no-no at the *o.* Wait until you're off the clock.
- Confess. Once you're an item, the right thing to do is tell your boss.[10]

PRISON LOVE

More and more women see loving a man behind bars as a viable option. It takes considerable effort to maintain relationships with men in secure containment facilities. One reporter went behind bars to study this growing trend. She discovered that many women would write to a number of prisoners before they finally make a sustainable connection. They may even take on voluntary jobs in prison, or go on blind-date visits with men they know only by reputation.

Prison relationships retain the intoxicating elements present in every romance. The first endorphin-flush of love always involves a degree of transference; we all see our partners as we hope them to be, imagining that the love object embodies the qualities we crave. Woman with imprisoned partners have limited contact and need never move beyond this courting stage. The intense desire for each other need never translate to the ordinariness of sex and marriage. Generally, the women are decent and well-meaning, and it is easy to see why they find their relationships fulfilling. Their boyfriends spend their days exercising and their evenings writing letters and poems or trying to phone home. They are more compliant and attentive than they would be on the outside because the women send money, pay for their legal representation, and afford them the tremendous parole advantage of a permanent address.[11]

Tracey is in love with Ray who lives in a state penitentiary two hundred miles away from her. They have been a couple for three years and she is pleased with the relationship. They first made contact through correspondence. "And it blossomed from there," she said. Tracey can quickly and easily give the positives of loving a man in prison. "My lifestyle/routine did not have to change in order to be in a relationship with him. I have three kids and they take up a lot of my time. He does not take up that much time, which is a good thing. I am free to come and go as I please without regard to him. I don't have to worry about him violating my space or getting crazy if I don't do this or do that. And I have peace of mind. I don't have to worry; I know where he is," she explained.

Tracey talked about their intense relationship glowingly. "I receive the most beautiful love letters. When I read them, I laugh, cry, and more. It seems our communication is more open than it is when we are face to face. Letters give us time to think beforehand. I think being locked up has made him more sensitive to women. I have never met a man on the streets that has shown so much concern for me. He has become more spiritual. If he had not gotten locked up he might still be living the thug life. Now he realizes that God is the head, not the tail. It gives us time to get to know each other on a level other than sex. I hate to say this, but in general, the woman has the upper hand. If I don't want to be bothered there is nothing he can do about it (until he gets out)," she laughed.

She, however, also offered the truth about the other side. "My honey will have a felony record for the rest of his life, which will make it hard for him to find a job and housing whenever he is released. I only get to see him on the weekends if I travel hundreds of miles to visit him, under the careful watch of guards. The only communications we have outside of visits are letters. Inmates are not allowed phone calls. No physical contact! (That's a big one.) My friends, family, and acquaintances usually have a closed mind about him and that is tough because I want to share. He is not able to support me financially; in fact, he needs financial support from me. Prisoners are not paid for their labor in this state, which is modern day slavery. He cannot act on what he is feeling (show his love through gifts, sex, and so forth), so the woman does not know if her honey is being for real. It could all be a con (pun intended). Some of these men will say whatever they must to keep you on their string."

MEN TO AVOID

There are some men that you should avoid at all costs. No matter how much you pray and fast for them, they will not change. Numbers of single women wind up throwing their lives away attempting to change a man. Understand that some men are the marrying kind and some are confirmed bachelors for life, despite your best peach cobbler. They'd rather die than walk down the aisle and marry anybody. Churchwomen often see these men as a challenge and believe that God has given them the green light to transform lives. What God has done in most instances is given you a red light, a red flag, a red everything, which means stop and run the other way. These men are not worth the trouble. Leave the miracle work to Jesus!

Commitment-Phobic Men

A commitment phobic man is one who runs from intimacy. The closer he gets to you in a relationship the more uncomfortable he feels. He senses that he is losing his identity or that you will swallow up his power. Some commitment phobes feel smothered in a relationship and, as a result, go from woman to woman to woman. They often have very high standards to ensure that no woman can meet them. This gets them off the hook and keeps them on the hunt for Mrs. Right.

It can be very frustrating to date a commitment phobic man because he may give the appearance that the relationship is going well and that there may be increased commitment. In reality he may be the type of person who dates many women in one church in rapid succession.

Author William July calls bachelorhood the "male promised land." "Attaining bachelorhood ranks up there with a guy's other great life experiences such as getting his first car, his first sexual experience, turning twenty-one, and graduation."[12]

Per July, there is a category of bachelors known as stringers. "He may spend lots of time with you and make you feel good but he will never marry you. These are men who string women along and never offer any commitment.[13] Queens, you must learn to identify and how to handle this type of man before you spend too much of your precious time with him. He will reduce you to a whining, whimpering girl.

A pattern can develop with stringers that most of us have either been through or heard about. It's the guy who dates a woman for years and refuses to commit. They break up; he begins to date another woman and soon thereafter marries her. How in the world did that happen? The experts say that the woman who eventually married insisted *that they commit early in the relationship.*[14] In other words, if you let him get away with noncommitment, he may never commit.

Queens know the importance of commitment from a man. One caller asked, "Dr. Patterson, I've been waiting for seven years for my boyfriend to propose; I am ready to get married, but he is not. We used to talk about it, now he says if I keep brining it up, it will never happen. So I am scared to say something to him, but I am also scared that we may never get married. What should I do?"

I responded, "You have two choices; you can sit and wait silently, hoping that he will come around at his own pace. Or you can let him know how much longer you are willing to go on without a commitment. Yes, this is an ultimatum of sorts, but it shows him that you are serious about getting an answer. If he wants a future with you on your terms he will come around. If he does not want it, he won't. Let him go and move on with your life, and pledge to never give another man seven years of noncommitment."

Multiple-Women Men

Sure there were men in the Bible that had more than one wife—Jacob, Gideon, David, and King Solomon, for example—but that was then and this is now. Polygamy was a part of the Old Testament world, but I am convinced that it should not be a part of yours. One man and several women is never a good idea. There is a passage in Isaiah 4:1 that describes this terrible scene: "Seven women shall take-hold of one man in that day, saying, 'We will eat our own bread and wear our own clothes, only let us be called by your name; take away our disgrace.'" Even though this passage was written centuries ago, it has chilling similarities to today.

Author Audrey Chapman in her book *Man Sharing* explains how she first became aware of this gender imbalance. "I resolved not to share another woman's man. But later when I moved to Washington, D.C. (where the ratio of men to women was once alleged to be about one to seven), I saw women condemned to man sharing and aggressively competing for males who, overestimating their value, refused to make any commitments."[15]

Here are my top five reasons why you should not share a man:

- You deserve one man to yourself. You are an awesome woman, who has much to offer.
- Your self-esteem plummets when you share. You begin to feel that you only deserve a piece of a man.
- You are deprived of his complete attention. He is juggling you and others and you know this and accommodate his schedule. For example, maybe he can only fit you in at 10:00 P.M. on Wednesdays.
- You'll wind up competing and ultimately doing more destructive things. Natural curiosity and competition sets in and there will be attempts to learn the other women's names and cut in on their time, or outdo them.

Unsaved Men

I also love the advice from Kimberly Brooks, author of the book *He's Fine, but Is He Saved?* In this book Ms. Brooks uses three young women as characters; each has different modes of seeing men. The flesh leads one, one is a holy roller, and the other is somewhere in between.

She advises single women to determine if the man she is meeting is saved early on in the initial conversation. "If he is not in the Lord, I don't get into him. I ask this when they ask for my phone number.

If they are not saved, I am not about to be their messiah," she said. She urges other women, "Don't lower your standards. When you are vulnerable you may accept a counterfeit."[16]

Biblically we are advised to interact only with those who believe in our God. In 2 Corinthians 6:14 we read, "Do not be mismatched with unbelievers. For what partnership is there between righteousness and unrighteousness? Or between light and darkness?"

This may seem harsh and narrowly focused, but it is necessary. The primary reason is to keep your faith intact. Often a Christian woman assumes that she is strong enough to convert or bring into the fold a nonbelieving man. What can actually happen is that he pulls her out of the fold. A nonbeliever may challenge your faith and your love for him may cause you to leave God. I call this missionary dating, because the two of you spend the date trying to convince the other of the benefits of their perspective. Second, it is difficult to walk in the ways of godliness on a daily basis if the person walking with you is going in a different direction. Third, should you marry the unbeliever, the marriage will not be a Christian marriage and not blessed by God. If there are children involved they will be confused about which way to go. Fourth, you will be attending worship alone. I call that being S.O.S. or Single On Sunday. Every church has a cadre of women married to men who don't go to church. Sitting alone every Sunday, they can be mistaken for single women, but they are married. This is not what they had in mind when they married, but it is the fate they now live.

Tiffany had an interesting situation. The guy at her office that she'd been hoping would notice her finally noticed her! He invited her out to dinner and she readily accepted. When he told her that he was taking her to the most expensive restaurant in town, she was ecstatic. Once they arrived he told her to order whatever she wanted from the caviar to the lobster, and happily she did. When the waiter placed the five star cuisine before them, Tiffany instinctively said, "Let's pray," and she bowed her head. Her date responded indignantly, "Don't you bow your head to pray to some damn God. I drove you to this restaurant and I am paying for this food. Get your priorities straight."

Violent Men

Violent men have a mysterious magnetism; women seem drawn to them because they can be very charismatic. Yet their charisma has a price, a painful price. Single women can become trapped in a relationship with a violent man and see no way out. She may not consider the violence to really be violence, especially if she is needy and dependent on him. The violence will not stop; only she has the power to stop it by ending the relationship as soon as possible. There are red flags in relationships that can clearly be seen. If any of these are taking place with someone you are dating, end the relationship as soon as possible. Does your partner:

- Embarrass you with put-downs?
- Look at you or act in ways that scare you?
- Control what you do, who you see or talk to or where you go?
- Stop you from seeing your friends or family members?
- Take your money or Social Security check, make you ask for money or refuse to give you money?
- Make all of the decisions?
- Tell you that you're a bad parent or threaten to take away or hurt your children?
- Prevent you from working or attending school?
- Act like the abuse is no big deal, it's your fault, or even deny doing it?
- Destroy your property or threaten to kill your pets?
- Intimidate you with guns, knives, or other weapons?
- Shove you, slap you, choke you, or hit you?
- Force you to try and drop charges?
- Threaten to commit suicide?
- Threaten to kill you?

If you answered 'yes' to even one of these questions, you may be in an abusive relationship. Attempting to love a violent man can have dangerous, lasting consequences. Here is one woman's story:

"My ex-husband and I dated a year and we were married a year. From the very beginning it seemed like he really wanted to be married. I had three children when we got married. However, as soon as we were married he wanted my children to be considered his children as well. He was a very good man, and he was a very successful man. Yet, he had one hidden problem. He had an issue with rage. I knew his mother had been in prison for a very malicious crime. She was later released and committed to an institution because the crime was related to an emotional disorder. I believe that my husband inherited that disorder.

"He was a very kind man, yet for no reason at all he would fly off the handle. It even got to the point of him being physically abusive. It didn't take me long to realize that he had a problem, but I could not stay around to wait for him to straighten it out. Shortly after we divorced he was murdered trying to help someone leave her boyfriend.

"His death, his birthday, our anniversary date . . . all happened within a ten-day time span. Even now as I think back on it, it is still painful. I finally got over the pain and have met someone who has been in my life for several years. Like my ex-husband he is very successful. But unlike my ex-husband he does not have an anger management problem. Any time I run into a man with a temper it immediately sends me a red flag."

In this chapter you have been given the tools to define men and not confine them. I hope that you have a queen's perspective on men. It's been a broad-based education. You learned to understand and appreciate the gender differences. You determined if you are a basher or a booster of men, and how to become a booster if you are a basher. You learned about platonic friends, office romances, dating men in prison, and what types of men to avoid.

Now you are ready to move ahead to even more intense education, dropping the drama in your life.

QUESTIONS FOR REFLECTION

1. When have you been a male basher?
2. How did it make you feel?
3. How do you handle the male/female ratio?
4. Why do women share their men?
5. Have you ever tried to change/save a man?
6. How do you respond to violent men?

PRAYER

Gracious God, thank you for creating good men. Please open my eyes to see them. Remove the obstacles that prevent me from acknowledging or appreciating them. I also pray that you keep me from dangerous, violent men. Surround and protect me with your love. Amen.

10 · DELIVERED FROM DRAMA

Hear me and hear me well. A woman can still be a queen despite the brutality of her past. Even if your yesterday was filled with pain, you will be alright, because the Word says, "Even though you intended to do harm to me, God intended it for good" (Gen. 50:20). There is healing available to all. The line of demarcation in life divides those who decide to receive the healing and those who do not. A queen cannot wallow in wasted lives. She refuses to marinate in multiple mistakes. She will not baste in brutish behavior. She makes up her mind that she cannot live like that any longer and rises upward. The ascent may take a while, but she is determined to move.

That's what I love about us—we will not stay down. If left unchecked, traumatic experiences can warp a life. Everflowing suffering can shut off hope. Nonstop bad news can cause bitterness. A queen sees herself as a victor and not a victim no matter what. In this chapter we will meet an array of queens who have been through the proverbial "hell and high water." They are queens because they moved through the trouble and did not set up house there.

In this chapter you'll meet Francine, who was delivered from prostitution; Felicia, who overcame a drug addiction; Monique, who escaped a violent relationship; Patti, who is an incest survivor; Marilyn, a breast cancer survivor; and Brenda, who was once married to a man living a double life. Let them show you how they did it. Listen to the bravery. Their heads are not bowed in the shame of their past. They know that looking down won't help them move ahead to their destination. They refuse to let yesterday's pain poison today. They won't be derailed, denied, or detoured by the past. I will move out of the way and let them tell their stories. They do it best.

LIFE AFTER PROSTITUTION

Francine, fifty-six, is a prominent minister with a past that she is not ashamed of. She matter-of-factly described her former life as a prostitute and stripper.

"It's hard for people to believe, but I was raised in a strict church. No makeup, no pants, and we stayed in church all day on Sunday. I've always been intelligent, but I had this thing in me that made me want to live on the wild side. I've never been afraid of wild living that had the potential to kill people. I liked money, and I talked good. It was a thrill to get men to pay me for conversation. When the enemy finds that in you, there is no limit to where you'll go. With wigs and clothes I created a new persona.

"I've been on my own since I was seventeen. My grandmother died and I got my own apartment. Instead of going to school I moved my boyfriend in. He dealt drugs and I started dancing in topless clubs. The enemy made it look very pretty. I had no shame in the fact that I was half naked in front of people. I went from dancing to meeting guys at the clubs, to getting money, to casual prostitution. Eventually that became too slow for me. The enemy made it look very pretty. I still went to church every Sunday.

"I glorify the deliverance that God gave me. God always has a hand in my life. God let me do my "thang" for a while, but I knew it was time to stop when I was asleep one night and I dreamed of a funeral. I looked in the casket and saw myself. When I woke up I promised God that I would never prostitute again. So I started to steal. I became a shoplifter and I decided to become the best shoplifter in town. I went to the best stores and stole the fanciest, most expensive outfits that I could. Eventually, I went across the nation doing wrong.

"I went to prison three times. The first time was aggravated robbery. After I got out, I went back on a probation violation nine months later. The third time I went back on another violation. The parole board said 'You are not here because you are illiterate but because you are rebellious against the system.' Due to the grace of God, they released me two weeks later. The day of my release, I got pregnant by my man at the time, a former pimp and a drug dealer. I had the baby, and have not looked back on that lifestyle."

Francine advises other women: "Don't keep your past private, the enemy will always keep you tormented. I tell people what God has done in my life. I am not ashamed. Don't try and keep it private. I saw an old john from my past and told him about my changed life. A few days later he called the church office hoping to embarrass me. But luckily I had already told my office about it. I will tell my own story. Shame over our past is why we can't help anybody; we are too caught up in what people think. I am not the one!"

She reflected on how she found blessing from the burdens of her former life. "My past impacts the way I interact with men. Back in the day I would dazzle them with conversation. I was a good listener. Now it plays a role in my discernment. All the men I've ever chosen were dogs. I was using body parts seductively. Now because I am not that person, I can quickly identify doggish men and I go the other way. I lean and depend on God. You are still flesh. I am very selective about who I date. I ask, what is really behind this dinner?"

Francine is adamant that queens should invest their deliverance in other lives. "I put my blessing to work on a constant basis. I now work with young girls, helping them to stay on the straight and narrow. I founded a ministry and a 501.C3 that allows me to preach, teach, heal, and evangelize the community seeking lost girls who are just like I was."

DELIVERED FROM DRUGS

Felicia is a recovering crack addict. At the age of forty-five she is a school receptionist. Her story is one of a hardscrabble life and a woman who refused to quit.

"Around age twenty-one, I used crack cocaine for the first time with no adverse affects. I must have done it wrong. I was told I swallowed the smoke. A year later, I began selling crack for a gentlemen much older than myself. Consequently, I decided I wanted to know why people kept coming back for more and more and more. I would make sure not to swallow that time.

"When I did try it again, I got a strong feeling of euphoria that only lasted for seconds after I blew out the smoke, thus causing the user (me) to want more. I was still not addicted. But it was so plentiful that I eventually got hooked. All I wanted was another hit so I could regain that euphoric feeling I had grown to love and hate. Smoking crack caused me to lose sight of my morals and values. I knew I was better than what I had become.

"I got real depressed and I made my first attempt to commit suicide by cutting my wrists. I was admitted to the hospital but assured them I was okay. A few days later, they let me go. After my second attempt, (this time by pills—cutting your wrist hurts), I was admitted once again for twenty-one days. I did fine for a while but eventually started smoking once again. I was admitted into a rehab facility for a month and stayed clean six months upon completion. I went to meetings for a while but got bored. And so many others were using crack around me it was hard to say no. I took the easy way out and gave in to temptation. I firmly believe crack cocaine is a demonic spirit and I was possessed.

"I tried getting my life in order once again by moving and not allowing my friend to sell out of my home. Then I met the man who would eventually become my third child's father. We smoked crack together. I paid the bills and we used his money to smoke crack. We had a good thing for a while, until I realized once again I was better than what I was and was becoming. I could not stand the sight of myself. I would smoke and read the Bible. Sometimes I would smoke while reading the Bible. UGH! As a result, I assumed the only thing that would make me stop harming my body was to have a baby. I pampered myself when I had my other two children and I didn't even plan them.

"Once I conceived my third child, I did really well for a while. In my third month, I relapsed. I knew then it would take more than my efforts so I turned to the Bible. That wasn't helping me because I didn't understand. I was just too simple. I wanted a step-by-step plan on what I was supposed to do."

Felicia also found herself addicted to men who were no good for her. "In my sixth month, I used once again and that was it. I had to go back to the church and leave my son's father alone. He was so cracked out he couldn't/didn't care about the baby or me. I went back to church but I couldn't stand the whispering and the looks. This is when I met one of the deacons, who took it upon himself to 'talk' with me. He encouraged and reassured me. I hate to say this, but my affair with this married deacon lifted my self-esteem to the point I thought necessary to continue facing myself and the rumors/gossip spread by church members and family."

She shared that her motivation to change was God. "The bottom line was that I was sick and tired of being sick and tired. Enough was enough! After I had my healthy, happy baby (yea!), the church started doing a study on the body, soul, and spirit. I felt like a whole new world had been opened up to me. I was learning why I did the things I did not want to do and how Romans 8 came into play. I learned the victory was mine when Christ died on the cross. I just had to get a renewed mind that told me I could not be defeated. I learned about God's love and putting God first. The rest is history. I went back to college and decided to move to a new state upon completion. I had a few relapses after the baby was born, but that teaching on body, soul, and spirit lifted me above crack cocaine.

LIFE AFTER DOMESTIC ABUSE

Monique, thirty-five, is a beaten woman who loved her abuser. Despite the blows to her physically and emotionally, she remained in a violent five-year relationship.

"I became numb as numb could be. I was flat. I did not want to feel anything. Carl had beaten the living daylights and nightlights out of me so many times that there was nothing left. I floated into a room, I was so light and lifeless. I stopped thinking too. I shut down completely. I don't know how my kids made it, because mommy was not there. The counselors said I had something called chronic traumatic stress disorder. They said that I had lost my soul, or what really happened is that I gave it to him.

"He told he that my thoughts were stupid. Pretty soon everything that I did was stupid. And because I was stupid was his reason to get mad and knock me against a wall. He said, 'Because you did this, I did that.' But knocking me down a flight of stairs over a comment was, like, everyday. He did a lot of bad things. He made me take out a tampon and prove to him that I did not have sex with anybody while I was at work. He brought in another woman to live with us, and made me a roommate. I stayed because I was a fool who loved him."

After a particularly violent night, Felicia and the kids went to a local woman's shelter. They wound up staying for six months. While there she learned a lot. "They counseled me and I figured out that my attraction to violent men was not happenstance. My mom lived with a man and had six children and never married, so I did not grow up in a stable home. The first man that came along and told me that he loved me, I went for it. I did not want to live in poverty, so a man seemed to be the good life."

Felicia gives God the glory for her new life. "Today I am away from him, and have my kids and a happy life. I am not interested in dating anybody right now. I just need time for me. I know it was God that kept me safe when we ran to the shelter. It was God that kept him from finding us. Now that he is gone, I can be the person God intended."

INCEST, LIFE AFTER THE PAIN

Patti, now thirty-nine, was a preacher's kid and the envy of many of her schoolmates. Her dad was the pastor of the city's largest congregation and she was given everything that she wanted from clothes to cars. She had it all. The ugly truth was that her life was not a dream, it was a nightmare.

"My dad started having sex with me from the age of eleven till eighteen. The most damage was done to my self-worth and self-esteem. It took away the thought that I could make choices of my own. I was not given a chance to make decisions as a girl. The assaults occurred when I was asleep. He would come into my room late at night. I had no choices over my body, so it carried over into adult relationships. I felt that I had no choice."

Patti explained how the incest made itself known in her adult life. "I was interested in a man if he was very aggressive and rough. He took what he wanted from me, be it sex, money, my car, and that's what I expected. I thought 'He must really like me, because he wants to have sex.'

"I did not start therapy until the age of thirty. I tried to deal with it on my own until I got to graduate school. I was forced to go because I was uncomfortable with myself. I was living unhealthy relationships over and over again. They were with the same type of guys, who were very similar to my dad. I was trying to fix them. In therapy I had to unlearn what sex was. My father had been molested as a kid too and I was so crazy that I was worried more about him than me. The little girl in me had to learn how to protect herself. I had to learn that I had the right to say no."

Patti explained how therapy helped prepare her for her fiancé. "When I met the man I am now engaged to, I did not like him at all. I did not appreciate him and did not understand where he was coming from. He was not all over me, he was taking things from me, and he was not calling me names. I thought he did not love me. If I had not been in counseling, I would have passed him by as a loser."

Patti's advice to other women who have survived incest: "Get the therapy. Don't try and pray this stuff away. It takes prayer and therapy. Do it for your future's sake. I did for the kids that I plan to have one day. I did not want them to feel my anger, abuse, and distrust. I did not want to be sexually abusing them. The pain of incest prohibits you from having a healthy relationship with God. Until then you can't access the love of God."

LIFE AFTER BREAST CANCER

Marilyn is a six-year breast cancer survivor. At forty, she looks good and feels good. Her cancer is in remission.

"When I was first diagnosed with breast cancer, I had my left breast removed. The very next year I had to have my right breast removed as well. As a woman, it was very difficult for me to deal with having both my breasts removed. It didn't take me long to decide to have reconstructive surgery to rebuild my breasts. I did this for two reasons. First I did it for myself, then for my husband as well. Yet, even though my breasts were rebuilt, it left me with a lot of scars in my chest area. As a result, my husband acted like it was very unattractive and he would not touch me. This caused me to feel rejected and later ended up dissolving our marriage.

"My ex-husband made me feel worthless after my surgery. His behavior played a major role in my lack of self-esteem and affected my desire to have a relationship with a man. Within no time, I built up a complex and became very withdrawn. Even when I was fully dressed, I believed that people could look through my clothes and see the scars on my chest. I cried to God to help me through this change. I did not want to be like this, but the flip side of the cancer would have been death. I knew I needed a better attitude about myself and about men.

"After my divorce, I did not date for a long time. I had to build up my courage to be with a man. When I finally decided to date, God blessed me with a man who was very patient. Now, I realize my biggest hurdle is not with men, it is with me. I have to get past feeling less than a whole woman. After I developed a spiritually intimate relationship with a man, it allowed me to realize that a man could love me again. It also helped me to respond favorably to flirtation and attention that I was given by men in public.

"I realize it may still be an ongoing struggle for me to be totally comfortable with my body. However, I am developing a genuine confidence in the woman God has created me to be, and I enjoy sharing that with the man who is willing to accept the woman I have become."

DOWN LOW MEN

A man on the down low is a man who lives a homosexual lifestyle secretly while maintaining a heterosexual image. Many women are fooled by these men, date them, and marry them. Brenda Stone Browder, author of *On the Up and Up: A Survival Guide for Women Living with Men on the Down Low,* offers powerful and pointed advice to single women. She was formerly married to J. L. King, a man who lived a down low life and wrote the bestseller *On the Down Low.*

"African American women are thirteen times more likely to contract HIV than their white counterparts. That can be directly tied to men lying about their sexual preferences. God delivered me from that situation. I could have been one of those women with HIV I saw being interviewed on CNN—women whose lives were ruined by the lies of men. The majority of women who are in relationships with men on the Down Low (DL) have no idea. In his book Jimmy suggests that there are no real signs to know if your man is on the DL. While I agree that there is not a way of telling just by a man's interest or the way he carries himself, I do believe that people living a double life throw off a certain kind of energy. As a follower of the Word, I do know there is such a thing as discernment. Use the insight and good judgment God gave you. If you get a bad vibe around someone and you have to constantly justify a person's behavior or attitudes to feel good about that person being in your life, you're probably better off without that individual. Don't ignore the signs. I did.

Brenda explained what some of the possible signs are. She also shared the extent of her denial. "In the dating world here are some signs: he is never accountable with his time, his behavior is inconsistent, his friends are a little too friendly and are always around. Among other things, I found a jewelry receipt for a piece engraved to his friend Melvin. There were nude photos of Jimmy taken by another man. There was pornography hidden away featuring men and 'missing you badly' letters from his 'friend' in Texas. Amazingly, despite all this Jimmy stuck to his lies."

Brenda offered powerful advice. "A DL man loves a woman who is not worldly and who will completely dote and depend on him. They want young girls, sheltered women who won't ask many questions and who won't hassle them. Be self-assured. Understand before you enter a relationship that you are fearfully and wonderfully made. I was young, naïve and in love with love."

SCRIPTURES TO STRENGTHEN YOU

These six sisters offered testimonies of the goodness of God despite the horrors found in our world. Their experiences would have destroyed weaker women. Now what about you? What drama in your life do you need to be delivered from? Meditate on the scriptures I've listed below and believe that God will bring you out.

Deuteronomy 20:1 "When you go out to war against your enemies, and see horses and chariots, an army larger than your own, you shall not be afraid of them; for the Sovereign God is with you, who brought you up from the land of Egypt."

2 Chronicles 7:14 "If my people who are called by my name humble themselves, pray, seek my face, and turn from their wicked ways, then I will hear from heaven, and will forgive their sin and heal their land."

Psalm 40:1–2 "I waited patiently for God, and God inclined to me and heard my cry. God brought me up from the desolate pit, out of the miry bog, and God set my feet upon a rock, making my steps secure."

Isaiah 43:18 "Do not remember the former things, or consider things of old. I am about to do a new thing; now it springs forth, do you perceive it? I will make a way in the wilderness and rivers in the desert."

Luke 1:37 "For nothing will be impossible with God."

2 Corinthians 4:8 "We are afflicted in every way, but not crushed; perplexed, but not driven to despair; persecuted, but not forsaken; struck down, but not destroyed."

Romans 9:38 "For I am convinced that neither death, nor life, nor angels, nor rulers, nor things present, nor things to come, nor powers, nor height, nor depth, nor anything else in all creation will be able to separate us from the love of God in Christ Jesus our Lord."

Philippians 4:7 "And the peace of God, which surpasses all understanding, will guard your hearts and your minds in Christ Jesus."

QUESTIONS FOR REFLECTION

1. Have you ever been hit by a man? How did you react?
2. Do you worry about others too much and not enough for yourself?
3. Do you consider therapy worth the cost and effort?
4. Do you love yourself despite your scars?
5. How much power do others have over your self-esteem?
6. Have you ever contemplated suicide? What happened?

PRAYER

Rescuing God, only you can deliver me from the drama in my life. It is not your will that I am surrounded by chaos and confusion. You are my way out of no way. Thank you for the testimonies of other women whom you have blessed. Please bless me too. Amen.

11 · MOMMA WANTS A MAN TOO

Single moms, you wear crowns when you balance self-care, concern for your child, and interest in a man. Otherwise, the crown comes tumbling off. It is difficult to balance all three, but not impossible. The desire for a man never supercedes the welfare of your child or self-care. A single mom has a real challenge in wanting a man and balancing her mothering skills. If she focuses completely on a man she may neglect her kids. If she focuses solely on her kids she may overlook or ignore the great guy in her midst. And if she focuses only on self, she may harm her child and never meet a good man.

The Bible presents images of mothers who are single usually due to the death of their husbands, for example, the widow at Zerapath and Naomi. One of the unusual single moms is Hagar, the Egyptian slave girl. Her story is found in Genesis 16:3–15, 21:8–21. I call her one of my favorites because she prevailed in the midst of difficult circumstances. We think we have hard times today. Well, compared to hers, ours look like a cakewalk. Hagar was a slave who was used as a surrogate mother by her owners, Abram and Sari. We do not know if she had a choice in the matter, but in most circumstances slaves had no rights. If the slave mistress was unable to bear children, it was the custom of that time that the slave woman bore children for her. The conception was successful, but things went downhill from there for Hagar. The slave mistress became insecure due to Hagar's ability to conceive, treated her harshly, and drove her away.

While she was on the lam, the angel of God spoke to her and assured her of blessings if she returned back to the slave owners. Hagar returned and bore a son. Eventually, more troubles arose and she was thrown out of the slave master's house and into the wilderness with her son Ishmael. Out of food and supplies, Hagar placed the boy a few feet away from her and wept. God responded with "What troubles you, Hagar? Do not be afraid; for God has heard the voice of the boy where he is. Come, lift up the boy and hold him fast with your hand, for I will make a great nation of him" (Gen. 21:17). The trials of parenting alone can make single mothers feel like Hagar, abandoned in the wilderness without the needed supplies or help. The answer is to cry out to God and know that God will answer. The Word gives us proof that God will make a way out of no way for single moms. I am very concerned about how you see yourself and how you see your sources of support. If you feel supported and undergirded, your entire life is different.

This chapter is designed to get and keep you balanced. First we will work on your relationship with God and your self-concept as a single mom. Then we will expand your base of knowledge regarding female-headed households, and from there we will look at maintaining concern for your children. This means understanding their emotional state and if need be safeguarding them from your negative emotional state. I also want you to see yourself as the faith role model for your child. Finally we move on to dating. There are helpful things to do and not to do to keep the crown on your head.

The first step in balancing is your relationship with God. Please don't consider your singleness a curse from God. You are not cursed, you are blessed. Do all that you can to celebrate what God is doing in your life as a mother. Watch and see how God moves through the lives of your children. Lift up your head during challenging times and wait on God. Hagar was amazed to learn that God actually saw her and that she mattered to God. When God rescued her this is what happened, "So she called the name of God who spoke to her, 'You are El-roi (God of seeing), for she said, "Have I really seen God and remained alive after seeing God?" (Gen. 16:13).

From a historical perspective you may not feel the confirmation because females heading homes have been much maligned. They are the target of poverty-related issues (blaming the victim for economic status while not acknowledging the role of social structure and accompanying inequalities) and often described as antimale matriarchs and welfare chasers.[1] In the 1960s, a report by renowned sociologist Daniel Patrick Moynihan concluded that African American families were "disorganized, pathological, and matrifocal." Families without two parents were labeled "deviant."[2]

It is never helpful to point fingers, blame, name call, or belittle female-headed households. Rather, I find the strength and dignity therein to help single moms be the queens they are called to be. Despite the negative press, there are positives about single, female-headed households. First let's change the terminology. The single female-headed household is not deviant; it is an alternative.[3]

Trinell, forty-eight, is a witness that single motherhood has its highs and it lows.

"I would have to say that it has been really hard at times. I conceived my first child while in high school at the age of seventeen. While everyone was going to the prom, I was sitting at home with a spoiled, sick child. My father was deceased and my mother disowned me. When some of my friends went off to college, I signed up for welfare and public housing. College was not something we were encouraged to do anyway.

"It was also no fun going to court to establish paternity. The deadbeat father stood up in court and said the baby was not his.

When I burst into tears, he later revealed he was stalling because he didn't have the money to pay. He later quit his job and moved so he wouldn't have to pay.

"Living from month to month on government assistance and without child support payments caused me to scrape by making ends meet. It upset me that I could not do this and that so I started going out a lot. I had so much responsibility that I started being irresponsible. As long as the kids were clothed and fed, I felt free to do as I pleased once they were asleep. Then too, I think I overcompensated my children being in a one-parent household by spoiling them and not being consistent with punishments.

"But . . . I also have some real good memories stored in my heart. Yeah, we struggled, but we prevailed. It feels good to look back and say, 'we made it.' My children are a crucial part of my life. If I had to do it all over again, I would have waited until I was older, but I can't say I would have waited until I was married. But that all goes back to one's values.

"What I'm trying to say is that even though I am complete in Christ, I feel like my children complete me and strengthen me when I am weak. They bring me joy and I wouldn't trade them for nothing in the world. Even my hardheaded son. I rest in the fact that everything happens for a reason. Having these children has made me the person I am today. And even though I could be more or less this or more or less that, I love me to be me."

Looking back historically, we can also see when the rise in female-headed households began. "The female-headed household became a common structures in the African American community from emancipation onward. Large numbers of children were not regularly found in such households. For example, in 1800, women between 30 and 49 years of age usually had one or two children younger than 18."[4]

A key to leading a balanced life is not to focus too much time and energy on the negatives. If we look hard enough we will find the positive—and there is positive data. Single, female-headed households generate a different gender dynamic, one that is more supportive of equal gender roles.[5] This means that children from single parent homes may lean toward less rigid gender roles and more equality in their homes.

- Single parent households are not a rejection of men or the devaluing of men. Being a single mom does not mean that the women are putting men down or doing without them. "The cause of the degradation of Black men is not Black women, but rather racism."[6]
- Single parent households provide models of support networks, familial and nonfamilial, which are essential to parenting. "The strongest models are African American single-parent families who have strong extended family patterns . . ."[7]
- Single parent households are often "models of independence, satisfaction, and strength.[8]

The balancing act begins with you. There are things that single moms need to do for themselves first. Noted author Marita Golden in her book on single motherhood, *A Miracle Every Day,* writes that, like her, other single moms must begin the inner journey. This is often more challenging because we don't enjoy inner work. It is often painful. "Many single mothers who work energetically and quite successfully to provide materially for their children, neglect their own emotional wounds, inflicting them on their children like a dreaded inheritance."[9]

What this means is that we are great when it comes to buying the shoes to cover the soles of their feet, but what about working on their souls? We have real work to do with our kids, but it begins with us first. Let me ask you. Have you handled your resentment at married mothers? Do you look at them and simmer because you have it so tough and they have it so good? Married moms are not the enemy. They are a part of your potential support network. If resentment is a part of your single motherhood it will be a bitter pill to swallow.

How do you handle your ex? Have you calmed down regarding your children's father? Single moms must forgive, forget, and release the drama if there was any with the father of their children. You cannot be a great queen of a mother and still keep up drama with the father of the kids. You owe it to them to be civil, cordial, and to some degree kind to this man if he is active in their lives. If he is gone, still resist the temptation to bad-mouth him. Work with him or the memory of him to ensure that your child has peace and harmony. Here is one mom's saga of anger at her ex.

"Yes, I hated Brian after the baby was born," Lisa shared. "I pressured him to marry me when I found out that I was pregnant and he made my life miserable every day that we were together. I could not have the baby and not be married, so forcing him seemed like the right thing. At least my parents were pleased. But the marriage was a mess, so I was happy two years later when he just suddenly left. It was one of the happiest days of my life. I felt free, about the baby and me. But it was funny—I wanted him gone from my life, but I never thought he'd leave his baby's life too. I guess I had a part in that. I kept the baby from him and refused to let him see her or even visit her. It felt good to make him beg. I finally had some control in the relationship. After a few months he stopped trying, but I had so much anger in me that I did not care."

In order for Lisa to truly be the queen that she is called to be, she must release the anger, forgive her ex, seek him out, and offer to let him see the child. It is the only way. Yes, her actions were in reaction to his, but the saying is true—two wrongs don't make a right.

Here is what is called the Most Wanted List for single moms. These concerns are noted for causing the most stress in single moms:

- Money
- Parenting relief
- Better housing
- Better relations with men
- A good job
- Concern over health matters[10]

You can turn this want list into a have list with planning, hard work, and perseverance. If more money needs to come into the household, consider taking on a small, part-time job that fits into your lifestyle, such as catering or baking.

Parenting relief comes once you have the guts to reach out and say, "Help; I need help." Sometimes pride will not allow us to reach out and instead we suffer silently. Don't be a silent sufferer. Let your church members and pastor know that you are in over your head. Make a phone call to a local support group or scour the papers for area single moms gathering.

If housing is a concern, do something about it by investigating new locations. If your current surroundings are not conducive to raising your child or if you feel unsafe there, don't wallow in your limitations. Pick up a newspaper and read the housing section. Get busy and search for a new and improved location.

If you hope to improve your relations with men, keep reading, and hopefully by the end of this chapter, that concern will be addressed. If a better job is on your want list, it requires the same initiative as the others. You've got to read the want ads, begin to network, and plan a pathway to the next job that you will get. And while you are looking ahead to where you wish to be, remember the great advice that says dress now for the position that you want to have. It will help you get there faster.

Concern over health matters is very serious, especially since millions of Americans live without health insurance. If your job does not offer it, you may want to consider getting it from an independent insurance agent so you can have peace of mind.

You already know that your past colors what's ahead, right? How you came to be a single mom has tremendous bearing on your present and your future. This is not an attempt to rate or judge the types of single moms. Whether you are a single mom due to the death of your husband or divorce or never marrying your child's father, pause and look at the impact it may have on your child. Queens are aware of that connection and work to make the best of whatever their situations with knowledge, prevention, and foresight. Following, I offer a few emotions that may occur. Each situation is different; this is only a guide.

If your children's father is deceased, have you and the children grieved his death or is there denial in place? Often children take their emotional cues from their parents. If mom has not taken the time to grieve, they will not either. Depending on the age of a child, the type of grieving will vary.

Grief experts suggest that we not put a timetable on the grief process with our children. Don't try and rush them through their time of sorrow. Understand that your child may exhibit physical signs of grief by losing his or her appetite, reverting to younger behaviors, and having difficulty sleeping. Be mindful of your own grief-induced mood swings. They may frighten your children. You can help them with their grief by planting a garden or tree in honor of the loved one. Or encourage them to write a poem about the memories of the loved one, or light a special candle to represent the love you have for that person, especially on holidays.[11]

If you are divorced from your children's father you and your kids may have a host of emotions ranging from anger to grief. Be aware of how you feel and how they feel. The experts say that there are at least five general concerns about divorce and children. Divorce can cause feelings of abandonment and insecurity because the nest of their family has been broken. Divorce affects the parent's ability to parent. They are understandably overtaken with the emotional work of the marriage. Divorce creates conflicts of loyalty in the children. They do not know whose side to take. Divorce can create an anxiety about the future in children. They see the future as unpredictable and may possibly develop phobias. Finally, divorce may create anger and resentment in the child towards the parents.[12]

If you never married the father of your children, your kids may be dealing with feelings of anger and abandonment. According to Jonetta Rose Barras, author of *Whatever Happened to Daddy's Little Girl?* such children may have fantasies of meeting/finding their father some day, or that he will come looking for them. Help the children not to see themselves as victims. Often fatherless girls feel unlovable and unworthy. They may fear commitment. "Consequently, in many respects the fatherless daughter becomes a dilettante, someone who passes through—floating but refusing to be touched deeply, because touch means involvement, and involvement means commitment."[13]

TAKING SPIRITUAL AUTHORITY

Queens understand the need to have not only parental authority over their kids, but also spiritual authority. They do not sit around waiting till a man is on the scene.

Single moms, I recommend that you become the faith role model for your children. Of course you have your pastor, but your kids should look to you for immediate spiritual guidance. You are responsible for their faith development. You should always have a scripture on the tip of your tongue or at least well marked in your Bible. In the book of Joshua we are reminded of the importance of preparing our children in their knowledge of God.

"When your children ask in time to come, 'What do these stones mean to you?' then you shall tell them that the waters of the Jordan were cut off in front of the ark of the covenant of God. . . . So these stones shall be to the Israelites a memorial forever" (Josh. 4:6–7).

This passage underscores the need to raise biblically literate kids:

- Teach your children to pray. When they are small is the best time, "because early childhood is a season of life when talking to God comes naturally and conversations aren't hindered by stilted language or ritual. Kids can learn to pray before they learn to read, ride a bike, or tie their shoes. They don't have to wait until they grow up and go to seminary to become an effective pray-er."[14]
- Make prayer time a routine in the home at bedtime, at mealtime, in the mornings, as frequently as you can. The Bible says, we ought to pray without ceasing. Guide them in praying not

just for themselves but for others as well. This prayer time with your children teaches them that God is aware of them and that they have the opportunity to reach out and communicate with God at any time. It also boosts their self-esteem to realize that they and not just the grown-ups can talk to God. It will also elevate them to know that someone as important as God is listening to them.

- Learn who your child is. Identify his or her gifts and personality type. Are they extroverted or introverted? Does math come easy or is dance her strong point? Your job is to know your child and groom the child. The parent should know her child and verbally praise and monitor those gifts and personality types. This also helps the child to know him- or herself.
- Don't hold on to anger at your child. If your son dented the car last month, don't hold on to your anger days and weeks later. It is childish and un-Christian to treat your child this way. It could evolve into withholding emotion and scar the child.
- Teach kids to say, "I'm sorry" and "I forgive you." As they hear you say it, they can say it too. When you are wrong, be quick to admit it and encourage them to do the same.[15]

Here's an additional one. Give your child a drug problem. Let them be able to say my mom drug me to church with her all the time. Studies show that children who are active in church have a much lower chance of getting involved in gangs, drugs or alcohol, or premarital sex.

MAINTAIN BALANCE

Single mom, your goal is to keep the balance of it all. Be aware that as you strive for balance, the pressure for companionship can have lethal consequences on the child. What does being out of balance look like? The next few paragraphs are disturbing, but they must be discussed in order that we know which way not to go.

Single moms who are out of balance may resent their children and see having a man as an escape from parental pressure. They may blame the child as the reason that they do not have a man. Headline after headline on the news tells the tragic story of yet another mother who has harmed, maimed, or killed her child. One mother was convicted of feeding her infant raw meat, hoping he would contract the deadly e-coli bacteria infection and die; when that did not happen, she went on to break all the bones in his arms and legs. Another mother placed heroin in her baby's milk bottle. She wanted to stop the crying; it was bringing down her high.

Sometimes the stress and strain of parenting is more than we can bear. Sometimes we snap under the weight of parenting and we hurt our kids. Harming kids can be generational. Persons who were abused by their parents have a higher likelihood of abusing their children. If you were emotionally abused as a child it is going to be extremely difficult for you to avoid repeating the kind of behavior that you experienced.[16]

Take the following questionnaire:

Have You Been Guilty of Emotional Abuse?

- Have you ever called your child demeaning names like stupid or loser or lazy?
- Have you ever made fun of your child's looks, intelligence, or other characteristics that he or she is particularly sensitive about?
- Have you ever ignored your child's request for help when he or she was crying, hurt, or frightened?
- Have you ever failed to show your child needed/desired affection (hugs, kisses, holding)?
- Do you sometimes make no attempt to monitor your child's whereabouts?

Avoid Physically Hurting Your Children

Experts say that if you were physically abused as a child or if you are a battered spouse, the most important things you must do to avoid physically abusing your children are:

- Determine that you will never use any form of physical discipline on your children. Your anger at being physically abused may be triggered as you discipline your child and a rage may occur.
- Develop alternative ways of disciplining your children that are fair and consistent.
- Find constructive ways of releasing your anger.
- Practice stress reduction techniques to help you stay calm around your children.
- Don't be ashamed of needing time away from your children in order to cool off.

Avoid Sexually Abusing Children

"No one who has been sexually abused is immune. The shame surrounding child sexual abuse—both the shame that you no doubt carry and the shame the perpetrator projected onto you—can sometimes overwhelm you to the point that you feel compelled to reenact your own abuse."[17]

- Know that these urges are very strong and overpowering.
- Start or continue to receive therapy. If not, denial of your own situation may prevent you from seeing the possible abuse of your child.
- Protect your child from others, checking in on them periodically.
- If you know that a child has been sexually abused, do not leave your child alone with that child.
- If your child is acting aggressively with other children, get him the help he needs.

If you have already become abusive with your children emotionally, physically, or sexually, it is not too late, says expert Beverly Engel.

"Although it certainly would have been better if you would have been able to begin your changes before you became abusive, it is never too late to change."[18]

Engel recommends the following steps:

- Admit the truth. Facing your reality is difficult, but it is the first step. Confession gives you the best chance at breaking the cycle.
- Seek help. Enroll in therapy, counseling, or a support group immediately. Don't try to help or heal yourself.
- Work on repairing the harm. This helps the victim stop blaming himself or herself and gives him or her a chance to vent at you and not other people.
- Acknowledge the harm. Offer a genuine apology for what you have done with no excuses. Make amends by offering to pay for therapy.

DATING AND THE SINGLE MOM

A common concern of single moms is, when do I date and how do I date? Is there a best time in the development of my child to seek a man? When kids are small, or in elementary school, or in college?

One mom may respond, "I refuse to date until my son is out of the house and in college. I need to give him all my attention and not divide it with some man. I'd be less than a good parent if I did not." Another mom may respond just the opposite with, "I am seeing a wonderful man and my parents keep my three-year-old twins when I go out. The kids head over there on the weekends, so I can go where I want to go. I get to let off steam from the week and so do they. It is a win-win situation."

There is no chronological best time for a single mom to date. Her best time is when she and the child are ready. Each mom must decide if her social life will help or harm her family situation at the moment. There is nothing wrong with dating or with devoting yourself to your child. When she feels ready, here is some dating advice.

Dating Advice

Do expect and prepare for questions from the kids about your date. It is not wise to keep them in the dark about your interest in seeing someone. Reassure them that you love them and it will never change.

Do not tell them too much about the person you are dating, such as intimate details or dating particulars. You must keep boundaries around your adult life and their lives as children.

Don't raise their hopes about your date becoming a potential father. This is cruel because it makes them look at every man and ask, "Are you my next daddy?"

Don't immediately bring your date to your house, or allow him to pick you up from the house. Meet him at a safe, neutral site until it's been six months or more and you are certain that he is worthwhile.

Do not invite your date to sleep at your house or let him stay there for a while. Under no circumstances should he become a part of your household unless a marriage takes place. This sends the wrong message to the children and opens them up to potential harm. It also undermines any attempt at teaching sexual abstinence to them by your example.

Sticky Dating Situations

Your children are trying to fix you up with every man that they meet. Not only is the embarrassing, but also it gives the impression that your kids think of you as desperate and needing their help finding someone. This could also be a cry for help for a male mentor or surrogate father in their lives. Talk with your pastor about a mentor program for the kids.

Your child demands that you stop dating. Some children are territorial and possessive about their parents. Any date may be instantly considered the enemy. They probably feel that they are losing you. Assure them of your love and that the date is not taking their place. Don't date to the detriment of the kids.

Your daughter flirts with your date. This could happen because she is innocently confused about how to behave around an adult male.

Or this could be inappropriate acting out due to anger. The flirting, especially with sexual overtones, may be an indicator of sexual abuse in her life.

The drama that you experience with men need not be theirs. Don't let the kids see you being made a fool of—if possible. One caller was a single mom with a desperate issue that impacted her and her kids.

Dear Dr. Patterson,

I'm in desperate need of counseling. My husband left me while I was at work. He was calling my job about a divorce, which had me tripping because I was a lead trying to be a supervisor at my job. I was the only woman on the dock. Well, about a year later, he was calling me saying he was sorry, and my stupid self, I loved him so much that I took him back. He came back cocky, disrespectful toward my things, and argumentative. Since I loved him, I tried to make him happy, but I found I was losing myself trying to please him. He wanted me to be his mother—you know, cooking, cleaning, plus sex, while I was working and going to school for medical insurance billing and coding.

When March came he asked me to marry him again. I said okay. Then he said he wanted me to put his name on the house. I told him I couldn't do that right now cause we are so shaky he might leave at anytime. Then I would have to sell the house. He said he wanted a place he could call his, which I could understand so I said if we could stay together at least three years I would do it, but we needed counseling. And I asked him was he going to pay the mortgage? He said he knew that's all I wanted. I was through walking on pins and needles. So I told him if he didn't pay it today he had to go 'cause I can't have a man living with me and not helping out. He had three paychecks and didn't pay anything. So he's gone.

He already had a place to go; that's why he didn't pay the mortgage. I feel stupid because I miss him and I know he's not the type to live by himself. He already had someone he was trying to get to. I NEED HELP about what do. I have to get him off my mind. I prayed about it, but I miss him. I'm sad, depressed. I wish he would just call and say he's sorry and he loves me and maybe I could leave him alone thinking he's missing me because I was a great woman to him. I need some counseling; can you help me?

Missing Him

Dear Missing Him,

Your ex has made a mess of your life. He has behaved poorly in the eyes of you and your children. The fact that you still want him indicates that you enjoy being mistreated. Your kids will learn from the both of you that negative behaviors should be tolerated. This is the wrong message. Seek counseling for yourself and the kids. It is best to move on without him, but you may need professional help to do so.

Another concern regarding balance centers on the men that we invite into our lives. Our dating demeanor need not be destructive. Momma's man can be the problem. He can be violent, a sexual abuser, a drug or alcohol addict, or more.

Cate invited Darnell to move in with her and her three kids after they'd been dating two weeks. Darnell was not the first guy to move in and he would not be the last, but he was different. What Cate did not know was that Darnell was a convicted sex offender. Darnell took an instant interest in the kids, boys ages three, six, and eight. He offered to give them baths, tucked them in at night, and encouraged his girlfriend to take those extra hours that were available during the graveyard shift at work. Cate felt relieved that she finally had a man who was about something positive. "I felt like I had a man who was about something. I felt comfortable at the job knowing that Darnell had the boys and was taking good care of them.

"Then suddenly, things just did not seem right. The boys became clingy with me. They did not seem to want to stay with Darnell. All I knew was that I was able to make some good money for the first time since I had the boys, so they were not going to stop me now. I just figured they were used to my being there and could not handle the change. Darnell was a good man and I was not going to let them mess this up for me."

The single mom must also consider what lies ahead should she marry. The blended family is a common one. She must be prepared to step in and parent children that are not hers. Here is one listener's dilemma:

Dear Dr. Patterson,

I became engaged to a man over the past Christmas holiday and our wedding is this July. My fiancé has an eleven-year-old daughter from his first marriage who has lived with her mother since their divorce. He has visitation every other weekend. This past week, his ex-wife informed him that he will need to take full custody of his daughter because she is unemployed. The problem is I can't stand to be around his daughter. She is very disrespectful towards me and pretty much rules him. When she is at his house; there are no rules, she can do what she wants to do. I've tried to talk to him about it and he said that's how kids are. I am confused. I really love this man, but his daughter would make my life pure you-know-what. Can you give me some advice?

Almost Step-mom

Dear Almost Step-mom,

What a tight squeeze you are in. There are so many dynamics taking place in your situation. First of all know this, your fiancé's daughter needs to be disciplined. If he can't do it, it will fall on you. Are you ready for that task? The girl's mom may react negatively to your disciplining also. And it appears that your fiancé is useless in this area.

Ask these tough questions. Do you love this man enough to take on an unruly child and the wrath of her parents? Is the love between the two of you ready for a child? Are you moving too fast? Would a nine- to twelve-month extension hurt or help the engagement?

I am praying for you.

All right, single moms, are you ready to put the crown on your heads? This has been a grueling chapter. It has been challenging and I hope that it stretched you a bit. The end result will be pleasing to God. In this chapter, we set the goal of getting and keeping you balanced. First, we worked on you via your relationship with God and your self-concept as a single mom. Then we expanded your base of knowledge about female-headed households. From there we looked at maintaining concern for your children. This meant understanding their emotional state and if need be safeguarding them from your negative emotional state. I also wanted you to see yourself as the faith role model for your child. Finally, we moved on to dating. Keeping the crown on will require you to walk even closer with God.

QUESTIONS FOR REFLECTION

1. Is your crown on, single mom? Why or why not?
2. What needs to change in your life?
3. Which areas are in need of balance, self-care, and consideration of your child or dating?

4. Have you ever been out of balance? How did you know? What did it feel like?
5. Are you the faith role model for your son or daughter?
6. Have you explored the impact of your type of single status and sought solutions?
7. If you are dating, is it helpful or harmful to your kids?

PRAYER

Parenting God, you know my struggles as a mother. I place my parental future in your hands. I want to love you, me, the kids, and a man if you send one. I know I can balance them all if I hold on to your unchanging hand. Amen.

12 · RULES FOR ROLE MODELS

Queen, your love of God, of self, and of others makes you a natural mentor for the young. You just can't help yourself when it comes to reaching out and being a blessing to a child or a youth. You realize that you are an automatic role model because God is doing great things in your life and you've got to share them. No, you are not perfect, but who is? You are a work in progress with a lot to share. It is unqueenlike to hoard those blessings. God has been too good to you, and there are too many youth needing someone to look up to.

The term "mentor" originates from Greek mythology's story of the one who guided Odysseus. The world has utilized mentors for centuries in the form of wise elders who shepherded the young. Mentors are not social workers or surrogate parents or saviors.[1] They are women who care enough to give of themselves. Webster's dictionary defines a mentor as a "trusted counselor or guide."[2] A mentor is one who cares about others and leads the way for them.

Although the word mentor does not appear in the Bible, biblically, Jesus is the mentor to us all. We are to emulate him in all we do. That's why the wrist bands that asked "What Would Jesus Do?" became so popular. In Matthew Jesus tells us, "Let your light shine before others, so that they may see your good works and give glory to [God] in heaven" (Matt. 5:16). This is the essence of being a mentor. You are allowing the light that God placed in you to shine on others' lives so it can illuminate their paths. Further mentor definitions come from 1 Corinthians 11:1: "Be imitators of me, as I am of Christ." Also, "Keep on doing the things you have learned and received and heard and seen in me, and the God of peace will be with you" (Phil. 4:9).

Taking the time to be a mentor is vital to a queen because it gives our lives meaning and purpose above and beyond that of having a man in our lives. The energy and time that we invest in the life of a young person is a healthy diversion from the manhunt. This pursuit is tangible, worthwhile, and godly. You are investing in a human being and your efforts will reap rewards of some type. Valerie admitted that mentoring probably saved her life.

"If it had not been for the mentoring program at the office, my mind never would have gotten off of Rickey and our relationship. I knew that he was no good for me, but I could not move on. I signed up for the program on a whim, but once I was paired up with my mentee I felt some type of connection. She needed somebody to care about her and I did not realize that I needed to be needed too. We worked on her school assignments and went on a group trip to the symphony. It was not a lot, but it meant a lot to me."

I strongly recommend that you mentor young women as opposed to young men because we can teach what we know best. Queens have always been leaders for the little girls. It's our responsibility. We must do more than teach them about clothes and makeup, we must be their relationship role models too. We've got to be careful that we don't use them as dumping posts for our pain, frustrations, and disappointments in life. The same lessons that we are learning for the first time at forty-five, they should master by the age of fourteen. Society will teach them to get a man at all costs. We know better. If they do not get a positive role model then they will get a negative one.

In this chapter, we will explore what it will mean for you to become a mentor, or what it will mean to be an improved mentor, if you already are one. We will look at the world of adolescent girls. It is a different world from our days. There will be questions to ask yourself before you decide to mentor. We will look at the benefits of two common forms of mentor relationships. I will share my experiences as a mentor. We will look at three types of mentors—the faith mentor, the career mentor, and the relationship mentor. In some instances you may be all three combined.

If you've never mentored before, I wonder if it is because you never felt like mentor material? Sometimes our battles with low self-esteem and feelings of low self-worth prevent us from reaching out a helping hand. By this point in the book, your self-esteem issues have been confronted. You've got to believe that you are mentor material. "When you choose to become a mentor to a young person, you must first acknowledge that you are worth the admiration of that young person and that yours is an example worth imitating."[3]

Next, ask yourself these questions to gauge your readiness. These questions come from Tommy Dortch, former chair of the high-profile group, 100 Black Men of America. This group has chapters across the United States that maintain a strong mentoring focus.

- Do you enjoy working with kids?
- Do you have the time?
- Do you know how to set boundaries?
- You are not a social worker or a savior.
- Are you living a positive life?
- What are you getting out of this?
- Do you have unrealistic expectations?[4]

There are two common forms of mentoring: one-on-one and group. Although they are different, they both offer interaction and satisfaction to the mentor and the youth. The choice is yours to decide depending on your style of helping and the amount of time that you have. In the one-on-one mentorship you focus on one person and pour yourself into her life. "Research shows that, when run well, traditional programs facilitate the development of strong mentoring relationships that are significant to both youth and mentor. Research further suggests that mentors who are able to develop close, supportive relationships with youth are able to make the most positive changes in youth's lives."[5]

There are additional benefits: strong relationships; friendship-oriented social activities like playing sports, talking, or having lunch together; developing close, supportive bonds with youth. And mentors are more likely to develop strong, long-lasting relationships with youth.[6]

The second common type of mentorship is the group mentor style. In the group style, the adult is linked to a group of young people and spends time with them in a group setting. In a time when volunteers are often scarce, this format has appeal because it provides youths with adults who might not ordinarily get together. According to research, both mentor and mentees benefit from the group method.

> Participants reported improvements in youth's ability to communicate and work with others, as well as improvements in youth's relationships with teachers, parents and friends. . . . Both the mentor and the youth's peers seem to play crucial roles in fostering these benefits. Mentors observe, encourage, and facilitate youth's interactions with peers in the group. These interactions, in turn, foster friendships in the group and help youth feel comfortable interacting with and meeting new peers. Both mentors and youth also provide participants with advice and feedback on their behavior and, in some groups, provide youth with academic help and learning strategies."[7]

MOST FREQUENTLY DISCUSSED TOPICS IN MENTOR RELATIONSHIPS

Youth's personal issues or problems

How things are going in school

How things are going in mentor's life

Fun things mentor would like to do with youth

Ways youth could improve their behavior or attitude

Youth's family or friends[8]

The world of adolescent girls is a whirlwind, fast-moving, emotion-laden, sexually saturated place. These ingredients have been foisted upon them by adults. They wrestle with issues ranging from the images of women in music videos to dating violence to the pressure to join a gang. Coming of age as an African American young woman is laden with stereotypes and innuendo carried over from the days of our enslavement in America says Dr. Gail Wyatt, author of the book *Stolen Women.* "Given our history and the stereotypes that proliferate about our sexual promiscuity, specific instruction is crucial to their sexual development."[9]

Some women may be reluctant to mentor girls because they believe that they are intruding on the sacred mother/daughter bond. This is not true. Even those mothers and daughters with excellent relationships need another voice. No parental relationship in and of itself is strong enough to see a daughter through these years.[10] The benefits of having a mentor are tremendous. It may come as a shock to those who are moms, but your daughters don't tell you everything. Mentors are called anchor points or neutral parties and they provide the outlet that girls need to navigate the world. "The development of a close emotional relationship with a caring, trusted older woman who isn't a parent is an essential part of the maturation process."[11]

There are at least thirteen crises that occur in the lives of young women that they may not share with their mothers. They are:

1. I had sex last night.
2. I had unprotected sex.
3. I'm pregnant.
4. I've been smoking for a while; everyone at school does.
5. I got drunk last night.
6. I want to kill myself.
7. I throw up after each meal.
8. My mom doesn't care about me; she's not interested.
9. I hate myself.
10. I want the pill.
11. He hit me.
12. (An older male friend or relative) keeps coming on to me/sending me love notes.
13. This guy made me do something I didn't want to do.[12]

The value of having someone else to talk to was illustrated clearly in a published conversation between rapper/actress Queen Latifah and seven teen girls.

Latifah: "I know body image is something that's very important when you're a teenager, so let's start by talking about how you feel about your bodies. Tell me honestly, do you love your body?"

Andrea: "I would change a lot of things about myself. I want bigger breasts and a bigger butt. I'm okay with my legs and my feet, but I would change my toes—they're short and fat . . ."

Latifah: "What makes you feel you need to be different?"

Andrea: "I see a lot of girls in the media with beautiful faces and long, straight hair. They have this mad Coke-bottle shape and I'm like, 'Oh I want to look like that.' I want to look like Angelina Jolie."

Latifah: "How real is the pressure to look a certain way or to be slim?"

Jayda: "I used to make myself throw up to be slim."

Janae: "My dad wants me to lose ten to fifteen pounds so I can run track, and I'm like 'What?'"[13]

I go into public schools to spread the message of what being a queen is all about. You are never too young for royal grooming. As a mentor, my passion takes me to one of the rougher neighborhoods in the city. I am drawn to the girls like a magnet. I pray that I can make a difference on many levels, and so I go regularly to help them the best way that I know—with me. I mentor a group of young women at an area high school. I adopted this group with the intention of mentoring them from the ninth grade until graduation. The goal that I have is to prevent teen pregnancy, by any means necessary. The school nurse's survey of the class indicated that five were already mothers and four were pregnant by the ninth grade.

Here is a typical mentoring session. The auditorium is filled with 150 ninth-grade girls buzzing with excitement. I believe that they enjoy our monthly times together as much as I do. They are a blessing to my life. They know that the topic is boys and being in love and that excites them more. A number of them already had a crash course on the topic. It may be too late for them; I hope that there will be some who will receive my advice.

Why am I there, when I have many, many other things to do? The girls need me and I need them. They need someone to talk to who is not bringing judgment and hysterical responses to difficult questions. They also need the correct information. Usually peers and friends at the mall don't have the information and data that is needed to make serious decisions about life as a teen. They need consistency from an adult. I make sure that my message stays the same each visit. I want them to be able to depend on my words and me. They need high expectations. The goal of finishing high school without a baby is a lofty goal. This particular high school has the highest rate of out-of-wedlock births in the city. My girls live in homes where their older, single sisters may have multiple children, where their father is absent because he is in prison or never married their mother, and their mother may have children from different fathers.

They help me make sense of all that is happening in our world. The rap music, the fashions, and the latest slang words offer insight into their world and what is important to them. I need them to help me gauge where our world is going. I've been writing about African American women and love since the 1980s. This fresh crop of young women brings the new trends and directions that need to be noted. I don't have to agree with them to appreciate their perspectives.

RELATIONSHIP MENTOR

Your role as a relationship mentor may be to help your mentee understand what is going on with her body biologically. The changes can be frightening. The rumors and ignorance about biology are just as strong. Sometimes girls' parents cannot tell them, because they were never told. One survey revealed that African-American women are less likely to be taught about sex by their parents than by someone outside the home."[14]

If they are not told the truth, they will believe the lies. For example, some young women are told the lie that young men will contract a disease called "blue balls" if they do not have sex regularly. Furthermore, the lie says it's your job to keep the man from getting blue balls.

Another lie that needs to be destroyed is that having sex makes them new and improved. I noticed that those that were sexually active in my group (they were proud to announce it) seemed to hold themselves in a higher status than the others. For them, sex was a status symbol. They were somebody now. "Because African American girls had so little factual information about sex, they anticipated that they would expect sex to be romantic. In fact, most girls generally expect that sex will be wonderful or that it will transform them some way."[15] We can demythologize sex and play down the transformation aspect of it with realistic expectations of what can and will happen during sex: the risk of HIV, sexually transmitted disease, pregnancy, and ruined reputation.

Girls' appearance matters greatly. Mentors can help them learn what to do with their ever-changing, ever-developing bodies. Adolescence is a confusing, overpowering, mysterious time when their breasts and behinds morph before their eyes and seemingly all eyes are on them too. "African American girls may begin to look more grown up and potentially more sexual at an earlier age than do their white counterparts. Since they appear womanlier, their emotional maturity is assumed to be equal to their physical maturity. More is expected of them as sexually mature teens, when in reality they may still be little girls."[16] This means that more is expected of us to help them know how to carry themselves, how to dress, how to enter a room, and more.

I shared with the group a saying that an older sister had told me once about how to dress. She said, "Baby, if you don't plan on serving dinner, then don't set the table!"—meaning how we dress and carry ourselves sets the expectation for every man who looks at us. "That's not fair!" they retorted in unison. "I know it's not fair; life is not fair, but it is real. We live in a day of double standards," I explained. "Unfortunately, what we choose to wear or not wear speaks for us. People judge us by our outfits. You may be a holy virgin, but if you are dressed like a whore, guess what? People will assume the latter."

The experts agree that they need such help. Whether she knows it or not, or whether she likes it or not a girl makes a "sexual statement" every time she walks into a room that contains other people. Girls can find themselves pigeonholed by males (young and old) who make assumptions about sexuality based on the prominence of a young woman's breasts or other evidence of physical development.[17]

Relationship mentors can help the young women set realistic goals for themselves. If the girls can talk about their futures, they are more likely to work toward it. We once had an eye-opening session on marriage. I started the discussion on why I thought marriage was a goal for them. They quickly let me know that marriage did not work, was an opportunity for women to be abused, was designed to allow men to cheat, and was not a goal for them. What they did see as a possibility was a committed relationship, one in which the partners were true to each other until things didn't work out. As the mentor I had to accept their goal and not insist that my goal be their goal.

Relationship mentors teach healthy dating practices in ways they can understand. In my sessions, I strive to help the girls learn how to handle the men (boys) in their lives. The experts call this helping them to set a sexual protocol, which is how to pace a relationship in order to receive and maintain respect from boys.[18]

I told them one day, "If you don't learn how to handle the guys, they will handle you." This meant that now is the time to understand male/female interactions and realize the serious consequences. The name of that session was "How Not to Get Played," and we discussed scenarios ranging from what to do when you know that he is not telling you the truth to what to do when he is seeing other women and how to decide if it is worth it or not to confront the other woman. Confidently I shared, "If your boyfriend is cheating on you, it's time to cut him." I meant that it's best to end the relationship. Quickly I realized that my youthful audience heard another message. Many of them smiled and nodded their heads. "Yes, it is time to cut him, Dr. Patterson," they concurred. Then I figured it out. "No, I did not mean with a razor! I meant end the relationship!"

FAITH MENTOR

Depending on the location and restriction of your mentoring, you may be able to mentor a young woman in the area of her faith. Perhaps this may be through your church or community group or your family. As a faith mentor, you will help her learn how to cope with life through belief in Jesus Christ. "If your girl develops emotional coping tools more quickly with you than she would without you, she's better off learning from you sooner than later. With your guidance and support, she's less likely to engage in risky and/or self-destructive behaviors."[19]

Some youngsters grow up without any influence from the church. They grow up susceptible to negative influences and as prime targets from gangs. A faith mentor has a sacred trust that is built on the word of God. This mentor takes on the responsibility of showing the biblical way of life. Your actions and activities must be rooted and grounded in the Word.

"Without a spiritual identity, one that's right for them and of their own choosing, girls often find it difficult to confront the risks that are part and parcel of young adult life today. They don't develop belief systems that make sense for their own lives and their sense of self-worth often suffers."[20]

As a faith mentor you can:

- Encourage your mentee to attend religious services with her family or take her to church with you. Spending time together at church can be a bonding experience. If she is new to this setting, gently inform her of the sequence of events during the service. Don't take for granted that she knows the songs, ritual/liturgy, role of speakers or preachers, or the Bible.
- Share stories with her about your faith experiences. Open your memory bank and talk about what God means to you. Give her vivid examples of how you know that God is real and that Jesus is a healer and a restorer. These need not be preachy or condemning illustrations. Rather, they should be instructive and inspiring.
- Encourage her to join women's and girls' groups at church. If there are age-level or interest-appropriate programs at church, encourage her to join. These could include youth Bible study, youth retreats, women's and young women's luncheons. The fellowship of like-minded women will provide her with a community of believers.
- Lead her to appropriate Bible verses. Spending time in the Word with your mentee is crucial. She may not be very familiar with the Bible. You may not be either. Don't let that hold you back. Invest in a good study Bible or topical Bible for you both and start reading. Help her by offering powerful scriptures to read daily for strength.

CAREER MENTOR

As a career mentor you will help your mentee to see a larger job/occupation world around her. You will open doors to opportunity and exposure to job fields that she has never considered and could possibly point her in the way that she never dreamed she could go. Young women need us in this area because society can often send messages that tell them not to excel with their minds, only their bodies. Sometimes, smart, ambitious girls are looked down on, ridiculed, and suppressed.

Studies show that numbers of girls who achieved well in elementary school begin to slack off in junior and senior high school. Studies further show that their self-esteem begins to plummet at this time as well. This occurs for a number of complex reasons.

First their "emphasis during those years turns away from schoolwork and toward dating and interacting with boys." Second, "even the most well-intentioned female teachers often have the habit of calling on junior high and high school boys—who tend to be far more aggressive and forthcoming than girls of the same age—with greater frequency than they call on the girls of the same age." Third, "countless advertisements, videos, and popular magazine articles encourage girls to focus on boys, fashion, and sex to the exclusion of virtually any other topics.[21]

As her career mentor, spend time with her sharing how you made your career and education decisions. This may mean pouring over career journals and Internet sites to give her a broader perspective on what she can be. Help her create a plan to reach her goal. Step by step write down what she must do to get where she wants to go.

- Take her to meet a female local elected leader. Meeting the mayor, a senator, or a county commissioner, for example, is an empowering experience.
- Take her to hear a female motivational speaker to get her can-do momentum flowing. Such speakers usually have inspiring stories of overcoming great odds to achieve.

- Take her to your job for a day and let her see you at work. This may be her first time in an office building or in a professional setting and the beginning of a new reality for her.
- Take her to a networking event that's connected to your job. There is usually high energy at these events that is contagious. The women there are assertive and eager to get ahead in their careers. It is inspiring to watch them interact.
- Allow her to meet your circle of friends so that she can see groups of women heading in the same direction and know the power of positive peer support.
- Visits to a college campus can be eye opening for a young woman because they encourage her to start thinking about the possibility of attending an institution of higher learning. From the moment her foot touches the ground of the school she may be headed to a higher level.

Queens, you have an awesome, yet rewarding challenge ahead of you as a mentor. The young women of this world are crying out to us for assistance. All we have to do is be the wonderful women that God made us to be in order to make a difference. In this chapter we have explored what it means for you to become a mentor, or what it means to be an improved mentor, if you already are one. We looked at the world of adolescent girls, which is a different world from our days. I asked you questions to help you decide if you are ready to mentor. We looked at the benefits of one-on-one and group mentor relationships. I shared my experiences as a mentor. We looked at three of the ways of mentoring: faith, career, and relationship mentoring.

Queen, your journey is also complete. You have come a mighty long way and I am proud of you.

QUESTIONS FOR REFLECTION

1. How does mentoring help you remain or become a queen?
2. What is the role of your self-esteem in being a mentor?
3. Did you have a mentor as a girl/teen? If you how did it help you? If not did you miss anything?
4. How is the world of young girls different from your world as a girl?
5. Do you agree that every girl could use another mature woman in her life as a neutral party?

Prayer

Sustaining God, create in me the ability to mentor. Remove any selfishness or fear or procrastination that hinders me. Help me to connect with a young woman whom I can guide as you guide me. I need to be a blessing to others. Amen.

Conclusion

Have you enjoyed the journey with me? I certainly enjoyed traveling with you. Your joys are my joys. Your pain is my pain. Your accomplishments are my accomplishments. We are in this together. The challenges that I face as a servant of God take me into the lives of great people like you. Yes, I realize that I got all up in your business, but it's my job as the Love Doctor.

Got time for a final quick review? In chapter 1, I wanted you to walk away with the understanding that God undergirds your royalty and that you are to build a full life around that relationship with God. In chapter 2, I wanted you to wipe your slate off and invite God's heavenly cleansers in to get it together. It's easier than trying to mark over everything.

In chapter 3, I hoped that the cleansing spirit would carry over into your life and you'd scrub everything off around you. In chapter 4, I wrote that you might realistically look at why you seek marriage. If your reasons aren't adding up, put it on pause. In chapter 5, I got very personal and invaded your space. Forgive me, but it had to be done. If any of the problems described you, please seek immediate medical attention. In chapter 6, I took you to church and preached a little. Those vignettes have enough "Amen" in them to get you through tough times. In chapter 7, I extolled the value of a friend and helped you to see their value in your life. In chapter 8, I began a two-chapter focus on men. The goal was to promote peace.

Queens have a role in creating harmony between the genders. In chapter 9, the exploration of men was continued for your empowering and enlightenment. In chapter 10, you met six queens who came out of the fires of life and did not get burned. In chapter 11, single moms were spotlighted and shown how they can have it all—in the name of Jesus. In chapter 12 our obligation to future queens was presented. They are watching, so we must have ourselves together.

Your crown should be firmly placed on your head now that you have reached the conclusion of this book. Keep it there; that's where it belongs. You should be a different woman by now. You cannot be the same if you read, applied, studied, and implemented the information from this book. Now you understand what it means to be a queen in a world filled with women who are content to live beneath the promises of God for their potential. Now that you know, you've got to let the world know that you are a queen. They will see it in the way you walk and the way you talk. They will discern that there is something regal about your demeanor. The men that you encounter will see it too. Your queenly aura puts them on notice not to step towards you with anything less than the best.

Congratulations!

Endnotes

CHAPTER ONE

1. David Keirsey, *Please Understand Me II: Temperament, Character, Intelligence* (Del Mar, Calif.: Prometheus Nemesis, 1998), 4.

2. Karen Gail Lewis, *With or without a Man* (New York: Bull Press, 2001), 46.

3. Ibid., 43.

4. Ibid., 53.

CHAPTER TWO

1. Sheron C. Patterson, *The Love Clinic* (New York: Perigee Press, 2001), 23.

2. Lawrence E. Gary, *Black Men* (Newbury Park, Calif.: Sage Publications, 1996), 88.

3. "African American Healthy Marriage Initiative," brochure, Department of Health and Human Services, Washington, D.C.

4. Joan Hunt and Richard Hunt, *Growing Love in Christian Marriage* (Nashville: Abingdon Press, 2001), 8.

5. Michelle McKinney Hammond, *Secrets of an Irresistible Woman,* (Eugene, Ore.: Harvest House Publishers, 1998), 17.
6. Patterson, *The Love Clinic,* 53.
7. Stephanie Staal, "Warning: Living Together May Ruin Your Relationship," *Cosmopolitan,* (June 2001), 286.
8. Donna Marie Williams, *Sensual Celibacy,* (New York: Simon & Schuster, 1999), 39.
9. Ibid., 129.

CHAPTER THREE

1. Michael Moore, "Coping with Toxic People," website: breakups 101.com/toxicpeople.html.
2. Ibid.
3. Jan Yager, *When Friendship Hurts: How to Deal with Friends Who Betray, Abandon, or Wound You* (New York: Simon & Schuster, 2002), 128.
4. Loriann Hoff Oberlin, *Surviving Separation and Divorce* (Holbrook, Mass.: Adams Media, 2000), 223.
5. Ibid.
6. Ibid.
7. Althea Lenore Honegan, "Surviving Divorce," *Essence* (April 2005), 117.
8. *The Book of Discipline of the United Methodist Church* (Nashville: United Methodist Publishing House, 2004), 99.
9. Paula J. Caplan, *The New Don't Blame Mother* (New York: Routledge, 2001), 43.
10. Ibid., 37.
11. Ibid., 158–70.
12. Jonetta Rose Barras, *Whatever Happened to Daddy's Little Girl?* (New York: Ballantine, 2000), 68.
13. Peter Goldenthal, *Why Can't We Get Along?* (New York: John Wiley and Sons, 2002), 183.
14. Ibid., 33.

15. Robert L. Johnson and Paulette Standford, *Strength for Their Journey* (New York: Harlem Moon/Broadway Books, 2002), 20.

CHAPTER FOUR

1. Audrey Chapman, *Entitled to Good Loving* (New York: Henry Holt, 1995), 75.
2. Rachel Greenwald, *Find a Husband After 35* (New York: Ballantine Books, 2003).
3. Molly M. Ginny, "Single Mothers-to-Be Race Ticking Clock," *Women's eNews* (June 14, 2004).
4. Ibid.
5. Ibid.
6. Ibid.
7. Avis Thomas-Lester, "Single Women Becoming Moms," *Washington Post,* February 10, 2003, B01.
8. Ibid.
9. Chapman, *Entitled,* 112.
10. Debrena Jackson Gandy, *Sacred Pampering Principles* (New York: William Morrow, 1997), 24–25.
11. Joy McElroy, *Trophy Man: The Surprising Secrets of Black Women Who Marry Well* (New York: Simon & Schuster, 2002), 11.
12. Nailah Shami, *Do Not Talk to, Touch, Marry, or Otherwise Fiddle with Frogs,* (New York: Plume Books, 2001), 21.
13. Shewanda Riley, *Love Hangover* (Allen, Tex.: SunCreek Books, 2003), 168–69.
14. McElroy, *Trophy Man,* 11.
15. Cheryl D. Broussard and Michael Burns, *What's Money Got to Do with It?* (Oakland, Calif.: MetaMedia Publishing, 2002), 138.
16. Ibid., 145.
17. Marilyn Martin, *Saving Our Last Nerve* (Roscoe, Ill.: Hilton Publishing, 2002), 141.
18. Shirlee Drayton-Brooks and Neva White, "Health Promoting Behaviors among African American Women with Faith Based

Support," *The Association of Black Nursing Faculty Journal* (Sept.–Oct. 2004): 129–34.

CHAPTER FIVE

1. Shauna Curphey, "Black Women's Health Needs Unmet," *Women's eNews,* June 24, 2003.

2. Steven Friedman, ed., *Anxiety Disorders in African Americans* (New York: Spring Publishing, 1994), 27.

3. Curphey, "Black Women's Health," 1.

4. Ibid., 2.

5. Ibid., 3.

6. Marilyn Martin, *Saving Our Last Nerve* (Roscoe, Ill.: Hilton Publishing, 2002), 65.

7. David A. Seamands, *Healing for Damaged Emotions* (Colorado Springs: Cook Communications Ministries, 2002), 124.

8. Martin, *Saving Our Last Nerve,* 67.

9. Valerie Davis Raskin, *When Words Are Not Enough* (New York: Broadway Books, 1997), 54.

10. Ibid., 57.

11. Martin, *Saving Our Last Nerve,* 66.

12. Friedman, *Anxiety Disorders,* 109.

13. Martin, *Saving Our Last Nerve,* 70

14. Friedman, *Anxiety Disorders,* 110.

15. Angela Neal-Barnett, "To Be Female, Middle Class, Anxious, and Black," *Psychology of Women Quarterly* 24, no. 2 (June 2000): 129–30.

16. Ibid., 131.

17. Ibid.

18. Ibid., 135.

19. Ibid.

20. Jerome Taylor, Delores Henderson, and Bayle B. Jackson, "A Holistic Model for Understanding and Predicting Depressive Symptoms in African American Women," *Journal of Community Psychology* 19, no. 4 (October 1991): 306.

21. Stanton Peele and Archie Brodsky, *The Truth About Addiction and Recovery* (New York: Simon & Schuster, 1991), 189.

22. Ibid., 194.

23. Jill Westfall, "Society Doesn't See Addiction as a Disease," *Essence* (October 2004), 36.

24. Join Together Partnership for a Drug Free America 2006; www .drugfree.org/Intervention/Articles/SignsSomeone.

25. Peele and Brodsky, *Truth About Addiction,* 136.

26. www.stoppingovershopping.com © 2003 April Lane Benson, PhD. Used by permission of Dr. Benson.

27. Jane Burke, with Nancy Poole and Sue McGowan, "Women and Problem Gambling, The Women's Addiction Foundation website, www.womenfdn.org, 1.

28. Ibid.

29. Peele and Brodsky, *The Truth About Addiction,* 134.

CHAPTER SIX

1. Henry L. Masters, *Simon of Cyrene* (Portland, Ore.: Inkwater Press, 2004), 4.

2. Michael P. Green, ed., *Illustrations for Biblical Preaching* (Grand Rapids: Baker Book House, 1991), 200.

CHAPTER SEVEN

1. Karen Gail Lewis, *With or without a Man* (New York: Bull Press, 2001), 47.

2. Leigh Devereaux, "Loneliness," doctoral thesis, North Central University School of Psychology, date unknown.

3. Ibid.

4. Ibid.

5. Natalie Schwartzberg, Kathy Berlinger, and Demaris Jacob, *Single in a Married World* (New York: W.W. Norton, 1995), 118, 119.

6. Florence Issacs, *Toxic Friends, True Friends: How Your Friends Can Make or Break Your Health, Happiness, Family, and Career* (New York: William Morrow, 1999), 24.

7. Ibid.

8. Ibid.

9. Ibid.

10. Debrena Gandy Jackson, *Sacred Pampering Principles* (New York: William Morrow, 1997), 198.

11. From "Frequently Asked Questions," www.netaddiction.com. See also Kimberly S. Young, PsyD, *Caught in the Net: How to Recognize the Signs of Internet Addiction and a Winning Strategy for Recovery* (New York: John Wiley & Sons, 1998).

12. Jeffery E. Young and Janet S. Klosko, *Reinventing Your Life: How to Break Free from Negative Life Patterns and Feel Good Again* (New York: Plume/Penguin, 1994), 225.

13. Jan Yager, *When Friendship Hurts* (New York: Simon & Schuster, 2002), 157.

CHAPTER EIGHT

1. Sheron C. Patterson, *Ministry with Black Single Adults* (Nashville: Discipleship Resources, 1995), 31.

2. Carol A. Newsome and Sharon H. Ringe, eds., *The Woman's Bible Commentary* (Louisville: Westminster John Knox Press, 1990), 82.

3. Cheryl Green, *Worldwide Search* (Colorado Springs: Water Brook Press, 2004), xvii.

4. Ibid., xx.

5. Ibid., xvi.

6. Ibid., 7.

7. Mark Crutcher, *Checkmate* (Dallas: Drexell Publishing, 2003), 9, 10.

CHAPTER NINE

1. Christie Cozad Neuger and James Newton Poling, eds., *The Care of Men* (Nashville: Abingdon Press, 1997), 95.

2. John Gray, *Men Are from Mars, Women Are from Venus* (New York: HarperCollins, 1992), 69.

3. William July, *Understanding the Tin Man* (New York: Doubleday, 1999), 23.

4. Neuger and Poling, *Care of Men,* 96.

5. Ibid.

6. Ron Elmore, *How to Love a Black Man* (New York: Warner Books, 1997), 46.

7. Ibid., 42–43.

8. Ibid.

9. Ibid.

10. Mike Drummond, "Office Loves to Put It in Writing," *The Charlotte Observer,* February 14, 2005.

11. Denise Mina, "Why are Women Drawn to Men Behind Bars?" *Guardian,* January 13, 2003.

12. July, *Understanding the Tin Man,* 51.

13. Ibid.

14. John T. Molloy, *Why Men Marry Some Women and Not Others,* (New York: Warner Books, 2003), 12.

15. Audrey Chapman, *Man Sharing: Dilemma or Choice* (New York: William Morrow, 1986), 1.

16. Kimberly Brooks, *He's Fine, but Is He Saved?* (Detroit: Driven Enterprises, 2004). Radio interview, REJOICE Radio, February 2005.

17. ndvh.org/educate/abuse_quiz.html

CHAPTER ELEVEN

1. Bette J. Dickerson, *African American Single Mothers* (Thousand Oaks, Calif.: Sage Publications, 1995), 22.

2. Ibid., 23.

3. Ibid., 106.

4. Ibid., 22.

5. Nancy Dowd, *In Defense of Single Parent Families* (New York: University Press, 1997), 110.

6. Ibid., 108.

7. Ibid., 110.

8. Ibid., 105.

9. Marita Golden, *A Miracle Every Day* (New York: Anchor Books, 1999), 20.

10. Elizabeth S. Greywolf, *The Single Mothers' Handbook* (New York: William Morrow, 1984), 20.

11. Dr. David Stoop and Dr. Jan Stoop, eds., *The Complete Parenting Handbook* (Grand Rapids: Revell, 2004), 389, 390.

12. Ibid., 396.

13. Jonetta Rose Barras, *Whatever Happened to Daddy's Little Girl?* (New York: Ballantine, 2000), 69.

14. Stoop and Stoop, *Complete Parenting Handbook,* 156.

15. Ibid., 174–75.

16. Beverly Engel, *Breaking the Cycle of Abuse* (Hoboken, N.J.: John Wiley and Sons, 2005), 45.

17. Ibid., 199.

18. Ibid., 202.

CHAPTER TWELVE

1. Thomas W. Dortch Jr., *The Miracles of Mentoring: The Joy of Investing in Our Future* (New York: Doubleday, 2000), 7.

2. *Webster's New Collegiate Dictionary* (Springfield, Mass.: Merriam Company, 1977), 718.

3. Dortch, *Miracles of Mentoring,* 8.

4. Ibid., 40–60.

5. Carla Herrera, Zoua Vang, and Lisa Y. Gale, "Group Mentoring—A Study of Mentoring Group in Three Programs," report prepared for the National Mentoring Partnership's Public Policy Council. Funded by the U.S. Department of Education, Office of Educational Research and Improvement, February 2002, 75.

6. Ibid.

7. Ibid., 35

8. Ibid., 21, 75.

9. Gail Elizabeth Wyatt, *Stolen Women: Reclaiming Our Sexuality, Taking Back Our Lives* (New York: John Wiley and Sons, 1997), 103.

10. Pegine Eshevarria, *For All Our Daughters* (Worchester, Mass.: Chandler House Press, 1998), 3.

11. Ibid., 9.

12. Ibid., 13.

13. "The War on Girls, Lunch with Latifah," *Essence* (October 2002), 174.

14. Wyatt, *Stolen Women,* 199.

15. Ibid., 96.

16. Ibid, 93.

17. Eshevarria, *For All Our Daughters,* 5.

18. Wyatt, *Stolen Women,* 105.

19. Eschevarria, *For All Our Daughters,* 176.

20. Ibid., 221.

21. Ibid., 139–40.

Bibliography

"African American Healthy Marriage Initiative," brochure, Department of Health and Human Services, Washington, D.C.

Barras, Jonetta Rose. *Whatever Happened to Daddy's Little Girl? The Impact of Fatherlessness on Black Women.* New York: Ballantine, 2000.

Broussard, Cheryl D., and Michael Burns. *What's Money Got to Do with It?* Oakland, Calif.: MetaMedia Publishing, 2002.

Brooks, Kimberly. *He's Fine, but Is He Saved?* Detroit: Driven Enterprises, 2004.

Caplan, Paula J. *The New Don't Blame Mother.* New York: Routledge, 2001.

Chapman, Audrey. *Entitled to Good Loving.* New York: Henry Holt, 1995.

______. *Man Sharing: Dilemma or Choice.* New York: William Morrow, 1986.

Cozad Neuger, Christie, and James Newton Poling, eds. *The Care of Men.* Nashville: Abingdon Press, 1997.

Crutcher, Mark. *Checkmate.* Dallas: Drexell Publishing, 2003.

Curphey, Shauna. "Black Women's Health Needs Unmet." *Women's eNews,* June 24, 2003.

Devereaux, Leigh. "Loneliness." Doctoral thesis, North Central University School of Psychology. Date unknown.

Dickerson, Bette J. *African American Single Mothers.* Thousand Oaks, Calif.: Sage Publications, 1995.

Dowd, Nancy. *In Defense of Single Parent Families.* New York: University Press, 1997.

Dortch, Thomas W. Jr. *The Miracles of Mentoring: The Joy of Investing in Our Future.* New York: Doubleday, 2000.

Drayton-Brooks, Shirlee, and Neva White. "Health Promoting Behaviors among African American Women with Faith Based Support." *The Association of Black Nursing Faculty Journal* (Sept.–Oct. 2004): 129–134.

Drummond, Mike. "Office Loves to Put It in Writing," *The Charlotte Observer,* February 14, 2005.

Elmore, Ron. *How to Love a Black Man.* New York: Warner Books, 1997.

Engel, Beverly. *Breaking the Cycle of Abuse.* Hoboken, N.J.: John Wiley and Sons, 2005.

Eshevarria, Pegine. *For All Our Daughters.* Worchester, Mass.: Chandler House Press, 1998.

Friedman, Steven, ed., *Anxiety Disorders in African Americans.* New York: Spring Publishing, 1994.

Gandy, Debrena Jackson. *Sacred Pampering Principles.* New York: William Morrow, 1997.

Gary, Lawrence E. *Black Men.* Newbury Park, Calif.: Sage Publications, 1996.

Ginny, Molly M. "Single Mothers-to-Be Race Ticking Clock." *Women's eNews,* June 14, 2004.

Golden, Marita. *A Miracle Every Day: Triumph and Transformation in the Lives of Single Mothers.* New York: Anchor Books, 1999.

Goldenthal, Peter. *Why Can't We Get Along?* New York: John Wiley and Sons, 2002.

Gray, John. *Men Are from Mars, Women Are from Venus.* New York: HarperCollins, 1992.

Green, Michael P., ed. *Illustrations for Biblical Preaching.* Grand Rapids: Baker Book House, 1991.

Greenwald, Rachel. *Find a Husband After 35.* New York: Ballantine Books, 2003.

Greywolf, Elizabeth S. *The Single Mothers' Handbook.* New York: William Morrow, 1984.

Herrera, Carla, Zoua Vang, and Lisa Y. Gale. "Group Mentoring—A Study of Mentoring Groups in Three Programs." Report prepared for the National Mentoring Partnership's Public Policy Council. Funded by the U.S. Department of Education, Office of Educational Research and Improvement, February 2002, 75.

Hoff Oberlin, Loriann. *Surviving Separation and Divorce.* Holbrook, Mass.: Adams Media, 2000.

Honegan, Althea Lenore. "Surviving Divorce." *Essence* (April 2005), 117.

Hunt, Joan, and Richard Hunt. *Growing Love in Christian Marriage.* Nashville: Abingdon Press, 2001.

Issacs, Florence. *Toxic Friends, True Friends: How Your Friends Can Make or Break Your Health, Happiness, Family, and Career.* New York: William Morrow, 1999.

Johnson, Robert L., and Paulette Standford. *Strength for Their Journey.* New York: Harlem Moon/Broadway Books, 2002.

Join Together Partnership for a Drug Free America website: www.drugfree.org.

July, William. *Understanding the Tin Man.* New York: Doubleday, 1999.

Keirsey, David. *Please Understand Me II: Temperament, Character, Intelligence.* Del Mar, Calif.: Prometheus Nemesis, 1998.

Lewis, Karen Gail. *With or without a Man.* New York: Bull Press, 2001.

Martin, Marilyn. *Saving Our Last Nerve.* Roscoe, Ill.: Hilton Publishing, 2002.

Masters, Henry L. *Simon of Cyrene.* Portland, Ore.: Inkwater Press, 2004.

McElroy, Joy. *Trophy Man: The Surprising Secrets of Black Women Who Marry Well.* New York: Simon & Schuster, 2002.

Mina, Denise. "Why Are Women Drawn to Men Behind Bars?" *Guardian*, January 13, 2003.

Molloy, John T. *Why Men Marry Some Women and Not Others.* New York: Warner Books, 2003.

McKinney Hammond, Michelle. *Secrets of an Irresistible Woman.* Eugene, Ore.: Harvest House Publishers, 1998.

Moore, Michael. "Coping with Toxic People." Website: www.breakups101.com/toxicpeople.html.

National Domestic Violence Hotline website: www.ndvh.org.

Neal-Barnett, Angela. "To Be Female, Middle Class, Anxious, and Black." *Psychology of Women Quarterly* (June 2001): 129

Newsome, Carol A., and Sharon H. Ringe, eds. *The Women's Bible Commentary.* Louisville: Westminster John Knox Press, 2003.

Patterson, Sheron C. *The Love Clinic.* New York: Perigee Press, 2001.

______. *Ministry with Black Single Adults.* Nashville: Discipleship Resources, 1995.

Peele, Stanton, and Archie Brodsky. *The Truth About Addiction and Recovery.* New York: Simon & Schuster, 1991.

Raskin, Valerie Davis. *When Words Are Not Enough: The Women's Prescription for Depression and Anxiety.* New York: Broadway Books, 1997.

Riley, Shewanda. *Love Hangover: Moving from Pain to Purpose after a Relationship Ends.* Allen, Tex.: SunCreek Books, 2003.

Seamands, David A. *Healing for Damaged Emotions.* Colorado Springs: Cook Communication Ministries, 2002.

Schwartzberg, Natalie, Kathy Berlinger, and Demaris Jacob. *Single in a Married World.* New York: W.W. Norton, 1995.

Shami, Nailah. *Do Not Talk to, Touch, Marry, or Otherwise Fiddle with Frogs.* New York: Plume Books, 2001.

Shopping addiction website: www.stoppingovershopping.com.

Staal, Stephanie. "Warning: Living Together May Ruin Your Relationship." *Cosmopolitan* (June 2001), 286.

Stoop, Dr. David, and Dr. Jan Stoop, eds., *The Complete Parenting Handbook.* Grand Rapids: Revell, 2004.

Taylor, Jerome, Delores Henderson, and Bayle B. Jackson. "A Holistic Model for Understanding and Predicting Depressive Symptoms in African American Women." *Journal of Community Psychology* (October 1991).

Thomas-Lester, Avis. "Single Women Becoming Moms." *Washington Post,* February 10, 2003.

"The War on Girls, Lunch with Latifah." *Essence* (Octber 2002), 174.

Westfall, Jill. "Society Doesn't See Addiction as a Disease." *Essence* (October 2004), 36.

Williams, Donna Marie. *Sensual Celibacy.* New York: Simon & Schuster, 1999.

Woman's Addiction Foundation website, womenfdn.org.

Wyatt, Gail Elizabeth. *Stolen Women: Reclaiming Our Sexuality, Taking Back Our Lives.* New York: John Wiley and Sons, 1997.

Yager, Jan. *When Friendship Hurts: How to Deal with Friends Who Betray, Abandon, or Wound You.* New York: Simon & Schuster, 2002.

Young, Jeffery E., and Janet S. Klosko. *Reinventing Your Life: How to Break Free from Negative Life Patterns and Feel Good Again.* New York: Plume/Penguin, 1994.

Other books from The Pilgrim Press

INNER HEALING FOR BROKEN VESSELS
A Domestic Violence Survival Guide

LINDA H. HOLLIES

0-8298-1714-X/paper/112 pages/$15.00

Originally published in 1992, this book follows the healing process of the author as she made the decision to move forward with her life after being a victim of childhood incest. She outlines seven steps for healing.

LIVING BOUNTIFULLY
The Blessings of Responsible Stewardship

LINDA H. HOLLIES

0-8298-1676-3/paper/128 pages/$16.00

Jesus spent a great deal of time speaking to his followers about money and property. Hollies feels—like Jesus—that this is an issue that women in general and women of color in particular need to talk about and address in their personal lives. In *Living Bountifully*, Hollies shares her lessons, strategies, and experiences of godly stewardship.

ON THEIR WAY TO WONDERFUL
A Journey with Ruth and Naomi

LINDA H. HOLLIES

0-8298-1604-6/paper/130 pages/$18.00

This resource is an exploration of multicultural marriage (Ruth and Boaz) as well as diversity and racism in Scripture (God allows Ruth, a Moabite, to enter the forbidden Jewish bloodline). Women will relate to this book as it touches on issues that impact their lives, such as making critical decisions, handling relationships, and renewal of self and soul.

BODACIOUS WOMANIST WISDOM

LINDA H. HOLLIES

0-8298-1529-5/paper/144 pages/$18.00

Hollies takes a look at the "bodaciousness" of women of color through biblical stories of specific women such as the "bent-over woman" in Luke 13, Queen Esther, Mary, and other unnamed biblical women. Each chapter ends with a " Woman Wisdom Speaks" quote from Scripture and "Womanist Wisdom" and "Bodacious Woman" words.

JESUS AND THOSE BODACIOUS WOMEN
Life Lessons from One Sister to Another

LINDA H. HOLLIES

0-8298-1246-6/paper/224 pages/$11.95

Linda Hollies serves up new spins on the stories of biblical women. From Eve to Mary Magdalene, portraits of the bodaciousness of the many matriarchs of the Christian tradition will prove to be blessings for readers. Study questions and suggestions providing examples of how to grow in faith and spirituality, and of courage are included at the end of each chapter.

TAKING BACK MY YESTERDAYS
Lessons in Forgiving and Moving forward with Your Life

LINDA H. HOLLIES

0-8298-1208-3/paper/192 pages/$10.95

"A must read book! Linda Hollies has successfully combined personal honesty and solid biblical storytelling to teach us how to forgive and let go of yesterday. . . . The prayers will inspire you. The principles will encourage you. The psalms will direct your path." Iyanla Vanzant, author *Acts of Faith,* talk show host of IYANLA.

MOTHER GOOSE MEETS A WOMAN CALLED WISDOM
A Short Course in the Art of Self-Determination

LINDA H. HOLLIES

0-8298-1348-9/cloth/142 pages/$21.95

Fairy tales will never be the same! Hollies retells classic fairy tales with a decidedly spiritual spin. She provides a guidebook for women at the crossroads of their lives while looking at biblical women. The result is a biblical approach to practicing the art of self-determination.

PILGRIM PRAYERS FOR GRANDMOTHERS RAISING GRANDCHILDREN

LINDA H. HOLLIES

0-8298-1490-6/paper/128 pages/$10.00

This book will inspire grandmothers and give them the encouragement and comfort they need for the unique journey of raising their grandchildren.